# ADVENTURE TREKS

# WESTERN NORTH AMERICA

## Chris Townsend

The Crowood Press

First published in 1990 by
The Crowood Press
Ramsbury
Marlborough
Wiltshire SN8 2HE

**British Library Cataloguing in Publication Data**

Townsend, Chris 1949–
  Adventure treks: Western North America.
  1. North America. Western North America. National parks.
  Visitors' guides
  I. Title
  917.04538

ISBN 1 85223 317 6

**Picture Credits**

Colour photographs by the author; all maps by Don Sargeant.

Typeset by Griffin & Reiver, Cheltenham, Glos.
Printed in Great Britain by MacLehose & Partners Ltd

# Acknowledgements

There are far too many people, both at home in Britain and during the walks themselves, to mention by name who helped make my treks in Western North America a success. My thanks to them all, but particularly to Scott Steiner who was my trail companion on the John Muir Trail and Bob Marshall Country walks and whose idea for a ski tour there first took me to the Canadian Rockies, and to John Traynor who in the time I have worked with him has always supported my long walks and provided me with back-up even though it has meant my disappearance from the office for months at a time.

I would also like to thank the guidebook writers whose works I used on the trail and from whom I have shamelessly pillaged facts and figures for this book. This especially applies to Jim Wolf for his Continental Divide Trail Guides, Thomas Winnett for his John Muir Trail Guide, the various authors of The Pacific Crest Trail Guides 1 and 2, and Brian Patton and Bart Robinson for their Canadian Rockies Trail Guide. I hope they are repaid by more people buying *their* books after reading this one.

Finally, I must thank the National Park and Forest Service staff in both the USA and Canada who create and preserve the parks and wildernesses, maintain the trails, build the bridges and generally make enjoyment of the lands under their control possible. Long may they go on doing so.

# Contents

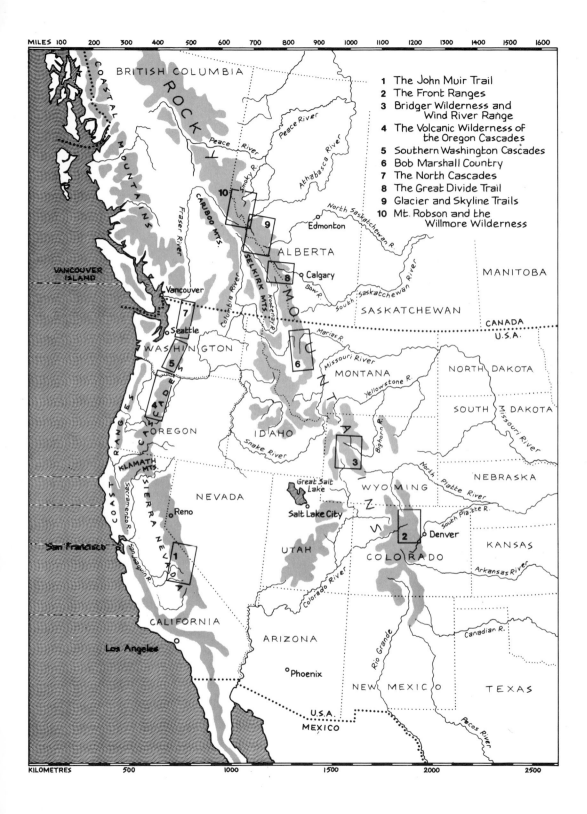

MILES 100   200   300   400   500   600   700   800   900   1000   1100   1200   1300   1400   1500   1600

BRITISH COLUMBIA

ROCKY MOUNTAINS

COASTAL MOUNTAINS

VANCOUVER ISLAND

Peace River

Athabasca River

North Saskatchewan R.

Edmonton

ALBERTA

Calgary

Fraser River

CARIBOO MTS.

SELKIRK MTS.

Columbia River

Kootenay R.

MANITOBA

South Saskatchewan River

SASKATCHEWAN

CANADA

U.S.A.

Vancouver

Seattle

WASHINGTON

Marias R.

Missouri River

MONTANA

Yellowstone R.

NORTH DAKOTA

SOUTH DAKOTA

Missouri River

CASCADE RANGES

OREGON

KLAMATH MTS.

Snake River

IDAHO

Bighorn R.

North Platte River

NEBRASKA

COAST RANGES

Sacramento R.

San Joaquin R.

SIERRA NEVADA

NEVADA

Reno

Great Salt Lake

Salt Lake City

UTAH

WYOMING

Denver

KANSAS

San Francisco

Colorado River

COLORADO

Arkansas River

Los Angeles

CALIFORNIA

ARIZONA

Phoenix

Rio Grande

NEW MEXICO

Canadian R.

TEXAS

U.S.A.

MEXICO

Pecos River

KILOMETRES   500   1000   1500   2000   2500

# Preface

'Travel' wrote Francis Bacon nearly four hundred years ago, 'is a part of education'. It is indeed, but it is also far more than that. Many – and not only altruistic dreamers – see the burgeoning travels of today's common man as an important key to international understanding and future world harmony. Others – more pessimistic yet perhaps more perceptive – see the profligate scatter of the tourist dollar as enriching local economies while despoiling subtle cultures and eroding fragile environments, a typical scenario in the Third World. There is much truth in both views. Travel is surely a two-edged sword.

Thus we who travel and enjoy the wild places – at risk by their very definition – bear a heavy responsibility. It is up to us to do the right thing, to set the right example, and back at home thoughtfully to champion the cause of the wilderness. It is all too easy to kill the goose that lays the golden eggs. The closure of the exquisite Nanda Devi Sanctuary by the Indian Government in 1983 is a case in point where excessive use, abandoned rubbish and environmental pollution had jeopardised its very essence.

*Leave nothing but footprints, take nothing but photographs* is a dictum originally coined in North America and usually pretty well observed in the impressive wilderness country that this book explores, where an educated public and an authoritative National Park system ensure that conservation and environmental considerations are treated seriously. But this very sophistication can lead to that characteristic pollution of the Developed World – 'people-pressure' – witness Yosemite Valley on Memorial weekend!

This book is one of the first of our on-going series of ADVENTURE TREKS titles which sets out to encourage the discerning traveller to undertake and enjoy journeys on foot – treks, hikes, walks, call them what you will – through many of the best locations for such activities among the world's wild places. The series covers regions of both the First, Second and Third Worlds (so called), typically in mountain or upland country because that is where the most interesting routes are usually found, and with difficulties and commitments to suit most tastes. It does so always mindful of the considerations discussed above.

Most travel books fall into one of two categories. Some are guidebooks pure and simple, usually useful and at best even interesting, if hardly a 'good read'. Others are narrative accounts, readable, fascinating, often extremely entertaining, but typically ignoring disdainfully any desire of readers to repeat the journey themselves. Hopefully the 'Adventure Treks' series embraces something of both, being entertaining and enthusing – albeit itchy-footedly – while helping the traveller with first-hand practical advice and crucial information.

Chris Townsend, the author of this volume, is a professional travel journalist and editor who, in ten years, has hiked more widely in North America than most native Americans. For this book he's selected his ten best routes – classic itineraries all – in the wild country that proliferates in the mountainous western regions of Canada and the United States. Take his advice and share his travels in the Wild West.

*John Cleare*

# Introduction

On reaching the pass the backpacker stops, any weary feelings from the climb swept away in an instant by joy and excitement as ahead there opens up an inspiring vista of vast conifer forests, shining snow-splashed mountains, curving cirques bright with flowers, dark blue ice-edged tarns, and the black and silver lines of creeks twisting through the landscape; a perfect wilderness untouched by human hand. Throughout Western North America there are areas like this, in which the walker in search of solitude and peace, challenge and adventure can wander for weeks without crossing a road or entering a town.

The Western Cordillera of North America is the evocative geographical name for the mountain ranges that run the length of the continent from Alaska to Mexico. South of Alaska and the Yukon the cordillera consists of the Sierra Nevada, the Cascades and, most famous of all, the Rocky Mountains. These are wilderness mountains with vast areas virtually untouched by human development even today. Unlike the Alps and other European mountain ranges and much of the Himalaya, the valleys of the Western North American wilderness do not harbour the settlements of generations of local people. Until the arrival of European settlers from the west, mostly within the last two hundred years, only small numbers of nomadic Indians roamed the mountains, taking no more than they needed and leaving little sign of their passing. As the European expansion coincided with the rise of the view that wilderness was worth preserving, there were soon calls for some areas to be left untouched and that led to the idea of national parks; the first in the world being Yellowstone in the Rocky Mountains of the USA. This ensured that the arrival of large populations, the introduction of agriculture and the building of towns did not affect huge areas of unspoilt wilderness. Throughout the mountains of the western states and provinces of the USA and Canada there are national parks and wilderness areas and it is in these areas that most of the walks in this book are to be found. However, there are still large areas of unprotected yet unsullied wilderness with much to offer the walker, some of which are in dire need of statutory protection.

The lack of any permanent settlement in the mountains has left wilderness without habitations, where the only people you meet will also be passing through and the only buildings you see will be the occasional log cabin. These ranges are ideal for the backpacker who likes to be self-sufficient and the walker who seeks solitude and deep wilderness. Although many trails have been constructed, there is no hut system as there is in most European mountain ranges and there are no local people to be used as porters. Some walkers use pack animals, traditionally horses, but these days other animals, such as llamas, are used. As distances are great, with many areas being several days walk from the nearest road, and trails long, the walker who doesn't use pack animals will have to carry everything needed to survive in the mountains. Indeed, this is the land where the word 'backpacker' comes from. Day walks from a car or cozy base will not get anyone very far into these wildernesses. The rewards of this land, and they are great rewards, are for those prepared to make the effort to delve deep into the backcountry and meet the challenge of living for days and weeks in the wilderness far from the comforts of civilization.

The linear nature of the mountain ranges makes this ideal country for long trails, and several have been developed, two of which

(Above) At the start of the Moose River Trail.

(Right) The author looking back over Resplendent Creek on the Moose River Trail, after the ford.

(Below) On the Rockwall Trail.

stretch the length of the USA. The Pacific Crest Trail runs for 2,600 miles (4,160km) from Mexico to Canada through the Transverse Ranges, the Sierra Nevada and the Cascades. The Continental Divide Trail, still being developed, will run for 3,000 miles (4,800km) down the watershed of the country, mostly in the Rocky Mountains from Canada to Mexico. No similar walks yet exist in Canada, but it *is* possible to link trails in the Canadian Rockies to make long distance routes. I've walked the Pacific Crest Trail and an end-to-end Continental Divide route, plus a length of the Canadian Rockies trek. It is from these three trips, which involved more than 7,000 miles

(11,200km) of walking, that I have selected the routes for this book. These routes can be walked in times ranging from one to three weeks, so are suited to the backpacker who doesn't have the time or desire to stay in the wilderness for six months at a time. There is a great variety of scenery covered and all the walks have their own uniqueness, but they all have one thing in common; they all take the walker deep into unspoilt wilderness and the natural world of the forests and mountains, the home of wolf and bear. I hope this book helps you to experience and enjoy these magnificent mountains and also to realize how important it is to preserve them.

# Along the Range of Light – The John Muir Trail:
## Mount Whitney to Yosemite Valley   210 miles (336km)

*The Sierra should be called not the Nevada, or Snowy Range, but the Range of Light . . . the most divinely beautiful of all the mountain-chains that I have ever seen.*

John Muir   *The Mountains of California*

John Muir was a Scottish emigrant, brought up in eastern America, who arrived in San Francisco in 1868 and immediately headed into the Sierra Nevada mountains to spend most of the following six years living in Yosemite Valley. In 1889, seeing that the mountains he loved were threatened by logging and livestock, Muir began a campaign to preserve them that resulted in the establishment of Yosemite and Sequoia National Parks and the setting up of the Sierra Club, one of America's leading environmental and conservation organizations. The John Muir Trail was established in his honour and runs for 210 miles (336km) through the heart of the Sierra Nevada mountains.

At over 400 miles (640km) from end to end the Sierra Nevada is the longest continuous mountain chain in the USA outside Alaska and has an area greater than that of the Alps. In width it varies from 60 to 80 miles (96 to 128km). A great tilted block of granite, the range rises to a high point at Mount Whitney, which, at 14,494ft (4,348m), is the highest peak in the contiguous forty-eight states, and from where the heartland of the range, known

as the High Sierra, runs north for 150 miles (240km) to Sonora Pass. On their eastern edge the mountains drop away abruptly 10,000ft (3,000m) and more to the semi-desert Owens Valley, while to the west the range fades away more gradually into wooded foothills. The High Sierra is a land of ice-sculpted alpine splendour, golden granite peaks and spires splashed white with glaciers and snowfields, dark forested valleys and flower-rich timberline cirques, deep blue mountain lakes and tumbling white creeks, crashing waterfalls and silvery cascades, through which runs the John Muir Trail, a magnificent tribute to one of the founding fathers of the environmental movement.

The main crest of the Sierra Nevada is too rugged for a trail, so the route parallels the heights, crossing the spur ranges that jut out to the west by a series of 11,000–13,000ft (3,300–3,900m) high passes in between which it drops down into forested valleys, to low points at between 8,000 and 9,000ft (2,400 and 2,700m). This makes for a roller-coaster of a path which is not for those who don't like steep climbs and descents. *En route* the trail passes the twelve peaks that rise above 14,000ft (4,200m) in the High Sierra (six in the Whitney region and six in the Palisades) and traverses Sequoia–King's Canyon and Yosemite National Parks as well as the John Muir and Minarets Wilderness Areas and the Devil's Postpile National Monument. Wilderness per-

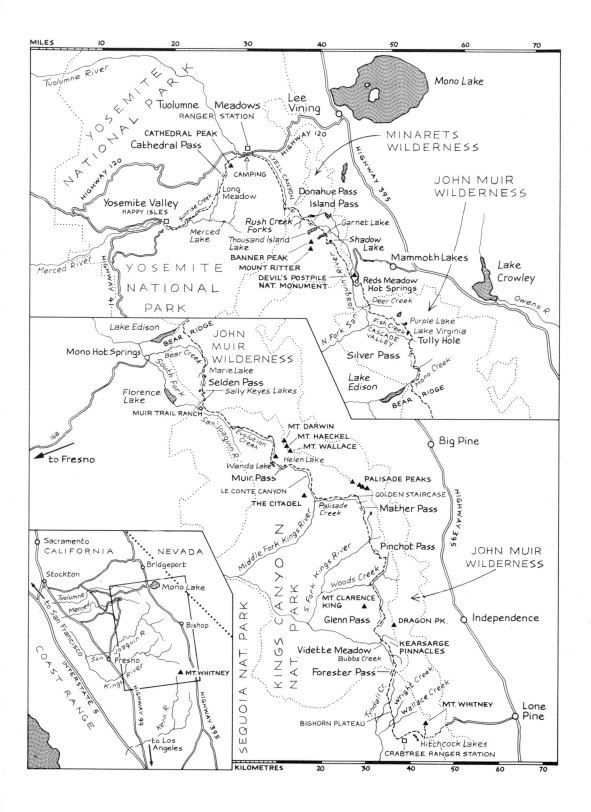

*The author on the summit of Mount Whitney.*

mits are needed for these areas, but you can obtain a permit that covers the whole of the trail from Mount Whitney to Tuolumne Meadows from the Chief Ranger's Office Sequoia–King's Canyon National Park, Three Rivers, CA 93271. For some reason you must say that you are walking the Pacific Crest Trail rather than the John Muir Trail to obtain this through – permit. In Tuolumne Meadows the ranger can issue you with a permit for the last section down to Yosemite Valley. As with most trails in the North American mountains, the John Muir Trail is a 'made' trail with carefully constructed switchbacks up the steeper slopes and even at one point a section, known as the Golden Staircase, dynamited down the cliffs of the Palisade Creek gorge. While the route is clear, trail junctions are often not signposted and many creeks are not bridged in keeping with land management decisions to leave the backcountry as free from human artefacts as possible.

The climate of the Sierra Nevada is possibly the most benign of any mountain range in the world. Between early May and the end of September the weather is mostly hot and sunny with only the occasional thunderstorm to break the monotony. This does not mean that the trekker should leave behind waterproofs and other survival equipment as the occasional cold front *does* track down from the northern Pacific to bring chilly, wet weather. The walker should also beware of sudden summer thunderstorms. These usually occur in the afternoon and are short-lived, but the rain can be heavy. Because of the danger from lightning it's best to be on the way down from high points, especially the summit of Mount Whitney, soon after midday.

Most people walk the trail during the holiday months of July and August. As the trail is the most famous and one of the most popular in America, it can be quite crowded during that time. You will meet other people on most days and share campsites most nights. This is not a midsummer trail for those who go to the wilderness in search of solitude. If you travel earlier in the season, however, you may not meet anyone. I walked the trail from mid-May to mid-June and met very few people along the way, but of course there are penalties with early season travel. I needed snowshoes, an ice axe and crampons to cope with the deep snow that covered much of the trail and a rope to safeguard creek crossings. It's not like this every year though. In *Pacific Crest Odyssey*, David Green describes walking the trail at the same time of year and finding virtually no snow at all.

Whatever time of year the trail is walked, the backpacker has first to reach the summit of Mount Whitney for it is here that the route starts. The shortest, most popular and probably most strenuous route is from Whitney Portal on the eastern side of the Sierra. From here a path climbs 13 miles (20.8km) and 6,133ft

(1,840m) to the summit of Whitney, a sudden gain in elevation that could well cause altitude problems and which will certainly require fitness as the walker setting out on it will have to be heavily laden. The first place where you can resupply on the trail itself is at Tuolumne Meadows, which is nearly 200 miles (320km) of walking away. Given an average pace of 12–15 miles a day that would mean starting out with 13–16 days' supply of food and a total pack weight of around 70lbs (31.5 kilos)! The only alternatives are to walk further each day, or to leave the trail and travel out to resupply, which is what I did and would recommend although it will add a couple of days to your total trek time. The walk takes from two to three weeks if you average 12–15 miles (19–24km) per day which will be quite enough with so much climbing involved. To fully enjoy the trail and allow time for the walk-in to Whitney

*En route to Forester Pass.*

and for going out to resupply I would recommend taking a minimum of three weeks.

One alternative to the abrupt start at Whitney Portal is to begin, as I did, at the Kennedy Meadows roadhead on the South Fork of the Kern River and then walk north for 60 miles (95km) along the Pacific Coast Trail to join the John Muir Trail at Crabtree Meadows. This adds three days or so to the walk, but it does allow for acclimatization to the altitude, which can be gained much more gradually, as well as being a spectacular walk in its own right. Crabtree Meadows, where there is a ranger station manned during the summer, lies 9 miles (14.5km) from the summit of Mount Whitney so the climb can be a day excursion; another advantage of joining the trail from the south.

The two approach routes join the John Muir Trail itself at the same point, just below 13,600ft (4,080m) Trail Crest on the main ridge of the Sierra Nevada from where there are wide-ranging and impressive views over the lakes, valleys and peaks of Sequoia National Park. From Trail Crest it's just 2 miles (3.2km) to the summit of Whitney, along a narrow and spectacular trail that winds across steep slopes a little below the main pinnacled ridge. At certain points there are sudden bird's-eye views through narrow rock-walled notches between the spires down to the pale red sands of Owens Valley, 10,000ft (3,000m) below to the east. With snow on it this trail can be quite a challenge. When four of us walked it in mid-May hard packed, steeply angled snow had built up below each pinnacle requiring care and the use of crampons and ice axes to cross safely. As I stared down between my legs to the valley floor far below I wished we'd had a rope and the means to set up belays. The sense of exposure was too great and the situation too airy for comfort and it was with relief that I reached the final broad summit slopes.

The summit itself is situated on a small plateau and marked by a plaque set in the rocks. Nearby is a small stone shelter hut and, out of place but necessary, a chemical toilet. When I was there there were no other people around, but in summer crowds can be expected. The view is wide-ranging rather than spectacular, as everywhere else is so far away and so much lower. You do get a sense of the vastness of the High Sierra and, looking at the endless mountains fading away into the northern horizon, the walker can relish the thought of all that lies ahead.

The trek along the John Muir Trail really begins on Whitney's summit so, as the first steps are taken back towards Trail Crest, the journey is finally underway. From the crest the trail drops in a series of rocky switchbacks 1,500ft (450m) into the valley below and then heads more gently downwards through an open alpine landscape to Guitar Lake and a good view of the steep north face of Mount Hitchcock. Soon after that, the first trees are reached and ¾ mile (1.2km) further along is the ranger station, Whitney Creek and Crabtree Meadows where there are many campsites.

Because we didn't want to repeat the icy traverse below the pinnacles, we descended straight down to the valley from the summit, glissading down one of the long, narrow gullies that reach down to near Guitar Lake. This is not to be recommended! We nearly came to grief here when Larry, who'd never glissaded or used an ice axe before, lost control at a narrow dogleg in the gully where rocks stuck up out of the icy snow and shot out of sight at high speed. Our other companions Scott and Dave had already descended safely so suddenly I was alone high on the mountain with the fear that Larry might be lying seriously injured or even dead somewhere below me. After what seemed an eternity of ominous silence a faint voice echoed up to me: 'I've lost my ice axe!' I scrambled cautiously down the loose rocks beside the gully to see Larry spreadeagled in the middle of the slope lying on his back. Crampons strapped to the outside of his pack had stopped his fall. I found his axe among the rocks beside the gully and slowly kicked steps down to him, not daring to glissade in case I slid into him. Shaken but with no injuries other than a badly grazed hand, Larry was then able to complete the descent in a more sedate fashion. Far below, Scott and Dave, unable to see what was happening, were waiting impatiently. I was relieved to reach the valley, feeling that we'd had a lucky escape. The nearest help was several days walking away so an injury would have been serious. Our round trip up Mount Whitney from Crabtree Meadows had taken thirteen and a half hours.

There are excellent campsites along the trail, but take care to ensure that the sites you use are left with as little sign of your stay as possible. Because the trail is so popular, many well-used sites are becoming eyesores due to over-use and careless camping techniques. Some particularly abused or sensitive places, especially lake shores, have been closed for camping and there are regulations governing where you can and can't camp, details of which are supplied with permits. Wherever you camp, no alteration of the terrain should be made which means no fire ring, trenches round tents, rocks on tent pegs, and so on. With such modern backpacking equipment as a stove, such practices are no longer necessary anyway.

Beyond Crabtree Meadows the trail wanders along around the timberline among some impressive foxtail pines, crossing two creeks which can be difficult to ford during the height of the snowmelt. My companions and I managed to find a snow bridge over Wallace Creek, the first of these. I then waded the second, Wright Creek, with my snowshoes still on! Beyond the fords there is a long climb up to the wide, flat Bighorn Plateau from where there is a dramatic view of Mount Whitney, and the long jagged ridges of the Great Western and Kings Kern Divides. A snow bridge again pro-

*A golden eagle.*

vided a way for me to cross Tyndall Creek at the end of the descent from the plateau. This can be a potentially difficult ford.

Next comes the climb to the first and highest of the series of passes that the John Muir Trail crosses, 13,180ft (3,954m) Forester Pass, which marks the boundary between Sequoia and Kings Canyon National Parks. Once the trees are left behind the approach is through an austere, rocky landscape dotted with mountain lakes, still frozen when I passed by. This is an appropriate setting for the pass which lies at the top of a massive granite wall that looks impossible to scale as you approach. However, a series of switchbacks, many cut into the rock, lead steadily up to the narrow windy notch of the pass. The upper section of these was still snow-covered during my ascent and at one point we had to cross a steep narrow ribbon of snow. Here I chose to climb straight up to the top of the pass not far above, but vertical soft snow stopped me a few feet from safety and I had to use our 5mm creek fording line and a belay from above to reach the safety of the pass. Such

foolish escapades are, once again, not recommended! The view from the narrow gap of Forester Pass is extensive and much of the country to be traversed in the days to come can be seen to the north. Switchbacks lead down the far side to Bubbs Creek though snow lingers here late in the year. This side is not very steep, so even when the trail is snow-covered as it was when I was there, the descent is not a problem. Once back down in the trees, Bubbs Creek is followed for a while and crossed several times. There are many campsites beside the creek, most with excellent views of the mighty serrated ridge of the Kearsage Pinnacles that lies ahead. In Vidette Meadows beside the creek there is a ranger station.

The pattern has now been set for the rest of the trail until the final descent into Yosemite Valley. It's like being on a giant switchback as the succession of wooded valley with rushing creek, bare lake-dotted rocky cirque, steep climb to high pass and descent to next wooded valley is repeated day after day. Yet every day is different, both subtly and on a grand scale. The cloud patterns, the types of trees, birds and flowers, the texture and colouring of the rocks all add up to make the walk a joy despite strenuous gasping climbs and cold foot-freezing fords.

A thousand feet above Bubbs Creek at 10,530ft (3,159m), after another steep ascent, Bullfrog Lake is reached. (It actually lies just off the main route along a short spur trail.) From here it is possible to descend to Onion Valley to the east via the Kearsage Pass Trail to pick up supplies either from the small store at the roadhead or, if you can get a lift, from the town of Independence in Owens Valley. Independence is where my companions went while I stayed with the tents and most of the gear beside Bullfrog Lake. I was there for three days, a peaceful interlude in the walk during which

*(Preceding pages) Silver Creek Falls.*

I was able to appreciate the more subtle details of the mountain landscape. I felt as though I could see the snow melting. Coyotes howled in the forest at night and the camp was visited by rosy finches, mountain chickadees and strident black and white Clark's Nutcrackers on the lookout for scraps. At one point a huge raven drifted by the tents, pausing to seize a morsel of food. Thick clouds on my second day at this peaceful site began to break up at dusk to reveal a yellow moon low in the bright pink sky.

My companions returned bearing welcome supplies and we left Bullfrog Lake for Glen Pass (11,978ft/3,593m) which, like Forester, is situated on a seemingly unclimbable wall of rock. A series of switchbacks takes the trail up this cliff, but as these were still plastered with snow we wore crampons to climb directly up a slightly less steep slope that brought us out on the narrow rocky ridge a few hundred yards west of the pass, along which we scrambled to the actual notch itself. To the north lay a steep descent and a monochromatic world of black rock and white snow. We glissaded most of the way down to Rae Lakes and a view of Dragons Peak and Painted Lady, two mountains banded by brilliant multi-textured red, gold and purple rock strata.

This long descent continues through the forest to Dollar Lake, above which we camped on a superb site with the wall of Diamond Peak to the east, the Rae Lakes peaks and soaring tower of Fin Dome to the south and jagged Mount Clarence to the west. Continuing downwards a magnificent forest of incense cedar, red fir and ponderosa pine is entered before the trail reaches a low point of 8,492ft (2547.6m) by the roaring torrent of Woods Creek which has to be crossed (for once there is a bridge). After the barren world of rock and snow, the richly coloured woods full of bird song, the bright green shoots of spring and the many butterflies made the Woods Creek valley seem quite luxurious.

From the creek, the trail climbs steadily all the way to Pinchot Pass (12,130ft/3,639m), an ascent mitigated, as most on the John Muir Trail are, by the wonderful scenery all around, especially the peaks that surround the glorious alpine basin immediately before the pass. A string of shining lakes is passed as you descend from Pinchot Pass into the broad valley of the South Fork Kings River. Climbing again alongside the river and past innumerable campsites, the trail heads into the Upper Basin, another alpine bowl where we camped, just below the last steep climb to (12,100ft/3,630m) Mather Pass. Because everywhere was snow covered, we actually climbed to the wrong pass the next day; an unnamed one east of and, regrettably, higher than Mather itself. Luckily, the far side was negotiable and led back to the trail beside Palisade Lakes. From the ridge itself we had a good view of the serrated 14,000ft (4,200m) Palisade Peaks. The lakes were still frozen on the last day of May so we walked right down the middle of them; the trail itself runs along the north-east shore.

The Golden Staircase comes next, a tight set of steep switchbacks built into the cliffs of the Palisade Creek Gorge that leads down to the forest. Below the Staircase the trail continues downwards, mostly through lodgepole pines, all the way to a low point of 8,020ft (2,406m) at the Middle Fork Kings River. Here, below the snowline, two mule deer crossed the trail in front of us, pausing to glance in our direction. The river is then followed upstream along Le Conte Canyon through Grouse, Little Pete and Big Pete Meadows. The canyon is impressive with many water slides and waterfalls, but there are also many avalanche chutes which can make progress difficult in early season as you struggle across the tangled mass of torn-down trees and hard-packed old snow. Trail crews come in and clear the route once the snow has melted. High above the timberline Helen Lake, named for one of John Muir's daughters;

is reached and we camped here at 11,595ft (3,478m), a bleak but grand site with views east to the Palisades.

Sitting outside the tent melting snow on my tiny stove I marvelled at the view and also at the continuous sunny weather. Even this early in the season afternoon temperatures were rising into the 20s°C (70s°F) and we were walking in shorts and tee shirts, but with gaiters to keep the snow out of our boots. However, at night the thermometer plummeted to −10°C (15°F) and I slept in my thermal underwear inside my summerweight down-filled sleeping bag and my Gore-tex bivouac bag even though I was in a tent. Mornings were the worst time as we rose before the sun to fumble with the stoves and try to don frozen boots and do up finger-numbing zips. It was hard to believe that we'd be too hot in just a few hours. Early starts were essential so that the steep climbs to the passes could be completed before the sun had softened the snow and created a danger of avalanches, and so that we could complete our day's walk by the middle of the afternoon after which time the snow became too soft for much progress to be made even with skis or snowshoes.

*John Muir Memorial Hut, Muir Pass, 11,955ft.*

*Camping below Muir Pass.*

Four hundred feet above Helen Lake is Muir Pass where there is a neat stone hut, the only man-made building open to walkers on the trail; this could provide emergency shelter, but shouldn't be relied on as it's quite small and could fill up quickly in bad weather. Muir Pass is the last point on the trail over 11,500ft (3,450m). An easy descent leads down via another series of lakes including Wanda Lake, again named for one of Muir's daughters, to Evolution Basin and Evolution Valley, where the surrounding mountains have names like Darwin, Huxley and Haeckel. The ford of Evolution Creek was just a knee-deep paddle although it can, at times, apparently be quite difficult. The long pleasant valley, dotted with meadows red and purple with the flowers of paintbrush and lupin, is followed for 10 miles (16km) before the trail switchbacks down steeply to the South Fork San Joaquin River. The river is crossed twice on sturdy bridges as the descent continues all the way down to

7,890ft (2,367m) at the junction with the Florence Lake Trail. Eleven miles (17.6km) down this trail is a roadhead and 1½ miles (2.4km) down it lies the Muir Trail Ranch to which food parcels could be sent. (Write to Box 176, Lakeshore, CA 93634 for details.) At the junction the trail starts a long ascent of the canyon wall to the north to timberline Sally Keyes Lakes where there are some good campsites. For the first time on the trail I felt here that I was on the edge of the mountains as I looked at the flat wooded hills rolling away to the west from the climb to the lake.

Shortly after the lakes lies Seldon Pass at 10,900ft (3,270m), beyond and not far below which is island-dotted Marie Lake, in the foreground of a panorama of rolling rounded mountains, less rugged than those to the south. From here onwards the scenery is more open, the climbs less steep and there are even more lakes in the wider, longer valleys. Down in the forest below Marie Lake, Bear Creek has to be forded. This was the toughest crossing of all on my trek and one on which we should have used the rope we were carrying. As it was, three of us shuffled across in a triangle formation through the foaming waist-deep, bitterly cold snowmelt water, just managing to keep our feet and feeling very relieved when we finally scrambled out on the bank. Canoeist Dave, well used to reading white water, had found a much safer crossing for himself. The only casualty of the risky ford was a camera lens which didn't survive an unplanned ducking.

It took some time before we warmed up after that ford as we followed the trail down beside the creek. Where the creek turns west, the trail climbs steeply up to the crest of Bear Ridge to a junction with a trail that leads after 6 miles (9.6km) to the roadhead at the Lake Edison dam. Four miles (6.4km) down the road is the post office at Mono Hot Springs (zip code 93642), the nearest one to the trail. As this is 115 miles (184km) from Mount Whitney, it's a good place to restock and is far less distance off the trail than Onion Valley. I wish we'd used it! From the ridge seventy switchbacks take the John Muir Trail steeply down for 2,230ft (669m) to Mono Creek which, at 7,750ft (2,325m), is the lowest point reached so far.

As always, a long descent means a long ascent and there is 3,320ft (996m) to be climbed between Mono Creek and 10,900ft (3,270m) Silver Pass. But this is spread over 7 miles (11km), so it is not too strenuous. During the steepest section however, on the canyon wall above the North Fork Mono Creek, the trail crosses Silver Pass Creek at a point above a steep cascade. The creek was in full spate and a fall here could be potentially fatal so we used our rope to safeguard the crossing. However as it was only 30ft (9m) long we had to belay in the middle of the stream on some water-washed boulders. For creek fords at least 60ft (18m) of rope is needed. Oddly the

trail does not go through Silver Pass, but climbs slightly further before dropping by a rather tortuous route to Fish Creek, a section of the trail lined with graceful mountain hemlocks. Here too I first saw the strange red spike of the chlorophyll-lacking Snow Plant which appears just after snowmelt and lives off decayed matter in the forest soil. Fish Creek itself is bridged shortly before the trail starts to climb again to the meadows of Tully Hole, a good place to camp, where we found just enough snow-free ground for our tents. The extra warmth and convenience of the bare ground was welcome. I was becoming fed up with the problems of snow camping; such as pegs that wouldn't stay in place and had to be buried deep in the soft snow of evening, stoves that melted into the ground spilling dinner in the process, the cold of the snow below permeating the tent, frosted inner walls dripping on me at dawn, frozen flysheets and zips freezing my fingers as I attempted to strike camp, and tent pegs that had to be prised out of the concrete-like dawn snow with an ice axe.

The long traverse above Cascade Valley and Fish Creek via Lake Virginia and Purple Lake to Duck Creek gives good views. Duck Creek is significant for two reasons. First, there is no water on the trail beyond here for 6 miles (9.5km) so in hot weather some should be carried. Secondly, the Duck Creek Trail can be taken for 6 miles to a roadhead and 6 miles down the road is the resort of Mammoth Lakes, a good place for resupplying. This is where I went out, hitch-hiking down the road to the town. Note, however, that just 11 miles (17.5km) further on is Reds Meadow where in the summer a small store can be found and from where you can also hitch-hike to Mammoth Lakes. Both this store and the road are closed early in the season (when they open depends on the snowmelt, in 1982 they were still shut on 9 June so the Duck Lake Trail was a better way into town). Mammoth Lakes is a sizeable ski resort with all facilities. It was twenty-three days since I'd left Kennedy Meadows, so I was very pleased to reach the town and have a shower and wash my clothes. Mostly though I just wanted to eat food that wasn't dehydrated!

The trail on from Duck Creek crosses the slopes of Mammoth Mountain as it descends to Reds Meadow, being joined *en route* by the trail from Mammoth Pass, which I took to regain the main route. As well as a summer store at Reds Meadow there are also year-round hot springs in which it is pleasant to soak aching limbs even if, as when I was there, the surrounding area is still covered with snow. Just past the hot springs is the Devil's Postpile National Monument, a huge cliff made up of vertical andesite rock columns formed during volcanic action similar to that which created Ireland's Giant's Causeway. At the base of the

*Bear bagging food at the Rush Creek bivouac.*

cliff is the 'postpile', the shattered remnants of broken and collapsed pillars.

The Minarets Wilderness is entered during the climb up from the Devil's Postpile to a traverse of the lake-dotted slopes of Volcanic Ridge, high above the valley of the Middle Fork San Joaquin River. The route through the terrain from here to Donohue Pass at 11,056ft (3,317m) and entry into Yosemite National Park is a complex one. Highlights of the section are the large Garnet and Thousand Island Lakes (the latter aptly named) and the constant views of Mounts Ritter (13,157ft/3,947m) and Banner (12,945ft/3,388.5m). Eventually the rocky trail crosses wet and wide 10,200ft (3,060m) Island Pass and then descends to Rush Creek at 9,600ft (2,880m), a creek that has to be forded several times. We camped by the creek before the first ford, preferring to cross early in the morning when the water would be lower. Even so the crossing was cold and thigh-deep. Four miles beyond Rush Creek, Donohue Pass, the last high pass on the route, is reached. To the north the peaks of Yosemite National Park can be seen, including the highest in the park, Mount Lyell at 13,144ft (3,943m), towering over the long dark gash of Lyell Canyon down which the trail runs for nine miles to Tuolumne Meadows.

As the long valley curves westwards, signs of civilization and heavy use appear. Multiple trails lace the flat grasslands and large campgrounds are to be found in the woods with steel cables between trees to hang food from, as the bear problem here is severe .The reason for the sudden increase in visitor numbers is Highway 120 which cuts through the High Sierra at Tuolumne Meadows at the far end of Lyell Canyon, the only road to do so. With the highway come facilities, including a store and post office and the Tuolumne Meadows Lodge which offers rooms, showers and meals. The store has an excellent selection of trail foods, unfortunately not really necessary for the trekker heading for Yosemite Valley, as there are only 24 miles (38.4km) left to walk. Note that the facilities here are seasonal, the opening date dependent on when the road is snowfree. In 1982 the store opened on 11 June, two days before I arrived. The large Tuolumne Meadows Campground lies ¾ mile (1.2km) off the trail, but most backpackers stay there.

Under the curving slopes of Lembert Dome, the sight of which confirms that you are in Yosemite, the land of domes, the John Muir Trail crosses the Dana Fork of the Tuolumne River and then Highway 120 as it heads west. I left the John Muir Trail here to continue north through the High Sierra on the Pacific Crest Trail, but for those completing the trail, the final 25 miles (40km) lead back across the highway and then south and west over Cathedral Pass (9,730ft/2,919m), and down the final long descent into Yosemite Valley and the roadhead at Happy Isles, the lowest point on the trail, at 4,035ft (1,210.5m).

# THE ROUTE

| MILEAGE/(KM) | | PLACE | ELEVATION | |
|---|---|---|---|---|
| | | | ft | m |
| 0.0 | 0.0 | Mount Whitney | 14,494 | 4,348.2 |
| 8.0 | 12.8 | Crabtree Ranger Station | 10,640 | 3,192 |
| 12.5 | 20.0 | Wallace Creek | 10,390 | 3,117 |
| 22.0 | 35.2 | Forester Pass | 13,180 | 3,954 |
| 30.0 | 48.0 | Vidette Meadow | 9,550 | 2,865 |
| 35.0 | 56.0 | Glen Pass | 11,978 | 3,593.4 |
| 43.0 | 68.8 | Woods Creek | 8,492 | 2,547.6 |
| 50.0 | 80.0 | Pinchot Pass | 12,130 | 3,639 |
| 54.5 | 87.2 | South Fork Kings River | 10,050 | 3,015 |
| 59.5 | 95.2 | Mather Pass | 12,100 | 3,630 |
| 70.0 | 112.0 | Middle Fork Kings River | 8,020 | 2,406 |
| 80.0 | 128.0 | Muir Pass | 11,955 | 3,586.5 |
| 93.0 | 148.8 | South Fork San Joaquin River | 8,470 | 2,541 |
| 99.0 | 158.4 | Florence Lake Trail | 7,890 | 2,367 |
| 106.0 | 169.6 | Selden Pass | 10,900 | 3,270 |
| 121.0 | 193.6 | Mono Creek | 7,750 | 2,325 |
| 128.0 | 204.8 | Silver Pass | 10,900 | 3,270 |
| 133.0 | 212.8 | Tully Hole | 9,520 | 2,856 |
| 145.0 | 232.0 | Deer Creek | 9,120 | 2,736 |
| 151.0 | 241.6 | Reds Meadow | 7,860 | 2,358 |
| 160.0 | 256.0 | Shadow Lake | 8,750 | 2,625 |
| 169.0 | 270.4 | Rush Creek Forks | 9,600 | 2,880 |
| 173.0 | 276.8 | Donohue Pass | 11,056 | 3,316.8 |
| 186.5 | 298.4 | Tuolumne Meadows | 8,650 | 2,595 |
| 193.0 | 308.8 | Cathedral Pass | 9,730 | 2,919 |
| 210.0 | 336.0 | Happy Isles | 4,035 | 1,210.5 |

From the summit of **Mount Whitney** (14,494ft, Mile 0), which is reachable via the Mount Whitney Trail from Whitney Portal on the east side of the mountains the trail descends south and then west to Whitney Creek and the **Crabtree Ranger Station** (10,640ft, Mile 8). Shortly beyond the ranger station, the trail turns north and climbs over a saddle before descending to ford **Wallace Creek** (10,390ft, Mile 12.5) and then, a mile further on, Wright Creek from where it climbs to Bighorn Plateau and then descends to the serious ford of Tyndall Creek. A long climb leads up to **Forester Pass** (13,180ft, Mile 22), then the trail descends into the Bubbs Creek valley which it leaves at **Vidette Meadow** (9,550ft, Mile 30) to begin the ascent to **Glen Pass** (11,978ft, Mile 35). From the pass, the trail drops into the Rae Lakes valley and then follows the South Fork Woods Creek to its confluence with **Woods Creek** (8,492ft, Mile 43), which is followed upstream to the climb to **Pinchot Pass** (12,130ft, Mile 50), from where it

drops down into a lake-filled valley that leads to the **South Fork Kings River** (10, 050ft, Mile 54.5). This is followed into the Upper Basin, from where a steep climb leads to **Mather Pass** (12,100ft, Mile 59.5) and a descent to the Palisade Lakes where the trail descends the Golden Staircase and turns westwards beside Palisade Creek. The trail turns northwards again at the confluence of Palisade Creek with the **Middle Fork Kings River** (8,020ft, Mile 70), the latter being followed up Le Conte Canyon to Helen Lake and **Muir Pass** (11,955ft, Mile 80). From the pass, the trail descends into Evolution Basin and then Evolution Valley, which is followed westwards to the **South Fork San Joaquin River** (8,470ft, Mile 93), where the trail again turns north to descend beside the river to a junction with the **Florence Lake Trail** (7,890ft, Mile 99). Here the trail climbs the canyon wall to Sally Keys Lake and then **Selden Pass** (10,900ft, Mile 106), and then descends to the Bear Creek valley which is followed until it turns

*Lembert Dome, Tuolumne Meadows.*

*View from the tent, camp below Muir Pass.*

west. The trail continues north to cross Bear Ridge and then descends via seventy switchbacks to **Mono Creek** (7,750ft, Mile 121), which is followed upstream to where it divides. Here the North Fork is taken as the trail climbs up to **Silver Pass** (10,900ft, Mile 128) which is not crossed. The trail instead continues northwards to descend through a lake-dotted basin to Fish Creek, from where it climbs to the grasslands of **Tully Hole** (9,520ft Mile 133). The trail then traverses the canyonside in a north-westwards direction high above Cascade Valley via Lake Virginia and Purple Lake, eventually turning northwards away from the canyon to cross **Deer Creek** (9,210ft, Mile 145), descending below Mammoth Mountain to **Reds Meadow Hot Springs** (7,860ft, Mile 151) and the Devil's Postpile. After crossing the Middle Fork San Joaquin River the trail climbs to a complex system of lakes which are passed before it descends to **Shadow Lake** (8,750ft, Mile 160). A climb leads to the larger Garnet and Thousand Islands Lakes and then Island Pass, before dropping down to **Rush Creek Forks** (9,600ft, Mile 169) and an ascent to the last high

pass of the route, **Donohue Pass** (11,056ft, Mile 173). The long Lyell Canyon is then followed to **Tuolumne Meadows** (8,650ft, Mile 186.5), where the trail turns west and then south to **Cathedral Pass** (9,730ft, Mile 193), Long Meadow and Sunrise Creek. A steep descent leads into Yosemite Valley where the trail ends at **Happy Isles** (4,035ft, Mile 210).

## MAPS

USGS 1:62,5000 topographic maps: Lone Pine; Mount Whitney; Mount Pinchot; Big Pine; Mount Goddard; Blackcap Mountain; Mount Abbot; Mount Morrison; Devil's Postpile; Mono Craters; Tuolumne Meadows; Hetch Hetchy Reservoir; Yosemite.

## RECOMMENDED GUIDEBOOK

*Guide to the John Muir Trail* by Thomas Winnett (Wilderness Press).

# The Front Ranges of Colorado: *Grand Lake to Silverthorne*
## 85 miles (136km)

*Wilderness is more than a physical place; it is a state of mind.*

Galen Rowell   *High and Wild*

The Colorado Rockies are at the southern end of the Rocky Mountain chain which stretches for 2,800 miles (4,480km) northwards almost to the Yukon. However, the chain is broken by the flat desert of the Great Divide Basin in Wyoming, a break that leaves the Colorado Rockies, which stretch the length of the state and on into New Mexico, as a separate mountain area with its own distinct character. An overlapping series of north-south trending mountain ranges makes up the Colorado Rockies, bordered on the east by the vast interior plains and on the west by the red rock deserts of Utah. The Continental Divide, the watershed of America, from which water running to the east ends up in the Atlantic Ocean, while that running west ends up in the Pacific, threads its way through these mountains before heading off into the flat desertlands of New Mexico. In northern Colorado the Divide follows the crest of the Front Ranges, so called because these are the first mountains encountered by the traveller heading west, a huge wall of peaks rising abruptly into the sky from the flat plains that lap their base. Fifty-four of these summits are over 14,000ft (4,200m) high, and are the highest in the whole Rocky Mountain chain.

However, for the walker who wants to travel along the crest of the range, along the actual Continental Divide itself, the central, slightly lower segment of the Front Ranges is the area to visit. Here it is possible to follow the skyline over five 13,000ft (3,900m) peaks, a glorious, but strenuous high level cross-country walk with spectacular views. Yet, amazingly, these mountains are not protected in a national park or wilderness area.

There are two possible starting points for a walk along the central Front Range, and two possible finishes. The heart of the route lasts just 38½ miles (61.6km), ideal if you only have a few days to spare, while the full route described here is 85 miles (136km) long, just right for a weeks' trek. There is much up and down on the walk, the majority of which is above timberline, with many high peaks and passes to cross, so this is a trek for the dedicated mountain hiker who likes to stride for miles along high ridges with wide-ranging views across the surrounding area. Because of the exposed nature of the terrain, and many of the campsites, this is a walk for fine weather. In stormy conditions it could be very difficult and, as much of it is on very sketchy trails or else cross-country, in thick mist care should be taken with navigation. There are only minimal facilities along the way, a café and tourist shop at Berthoud Pass, just over 52 miles (83.2km) from the start. It may be possible to send a food parcel here. (Write to Berthoud Pass Lodge,

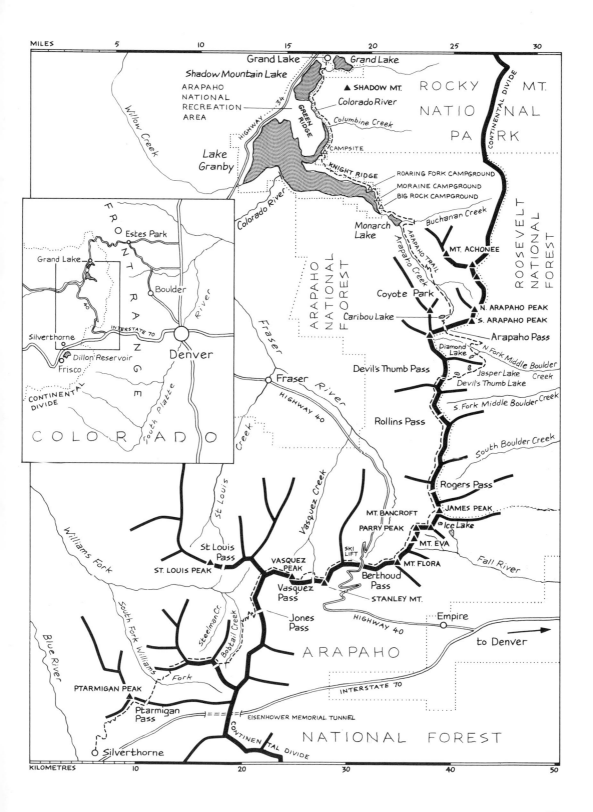

Box 520, Idaho Springs, Colorado 80452.)
Buses can also be caught at the pass.

The northernmost start point is in the pleasant little tourist town of Grand Lake, on the edge of Rocky Mountain National Park. From here a walk of nearly 14 miles (22.4km) takes you along the shores of Grand Lake and Shadow Mountain Lake to the gateway of the Indian Peaks Wilderness, so called because the summits in the heart of the area are named after Indian tribes, at Big Rock campground, the second possible starting point. A vehicle would be needed to reach the campground which lies at the end of a dirt road running round the other side of the lakes from the trail. As there is a steep climb immediately beyond Big Rock, I would suggest that those with plenty of time start in Grand Lake and use the walk by the lakes to break themselves in gently.

The approach route is mostly in forest, but with good views over the lakes. There are a few short climbs, and at the top of one of them there is your first sighting of the peaks around Arapaho Pass where the trail is headed. When I reached this point these peaks were ominously storm-shrouded, so perhaps for my peace of

areas, permits are required. These can be obtained as you enter the area and you do not have to say exactly where you plan to camp, you just state in which of the zones the area is divided into you'll be in each night. A few over-used areas, especially some lakesides, have been closed to camping. I picked up my permit at the ranger station at Monarch Lakes, less than a mile beyond the Big Lake campground. The ranger was very friendly and helpful and keen to describe the attractions of the wilderness and the many trails in it.

Beyond the ranger station lies the thickly wooded canyon of Arapaho Creek up which I started in cool, overcast weather on the signed Arapaho Trail. After a few bridged creek crossings the well-used pack trail starts to climb steeply, switchbacking up the canyon walls well away from the creek. As I climbed higher rain started to fall, which soon became heavy and cold. Struggling into my waterproofs I could hear thunder rumbling around the invisible peaks high above. Ten and a half miles (16.8km) after leaving the campground timberline is reached as the trail enters the large alpine basin containing Caribou Lake, at an elevation of 11,150ft (3,345m).

I walked into the full blast of the storm as I left the shelter of the forest and quickly reconsidered my aim of crossing Arapaho Pass, a mile (1.6km) and 800ft (240m) of ascent further on, that afternoon. Visibility was minimal and the wind was strong and cold; not good conditions for crossing a high mountain pass with no idea how far it might be to the next campsite. So, although it was early, I found a flat site protected by a few stunted limber pines and set up camp. As I pitched the tent, the rain turned to hail and then snow. By the time I was organized and inside, having left my pack with its cover on leaning against a tree and taken great care

mind it would have been better if I hadn't had the view at all. Two small lakeside campsites are passed, used mainly by boating parties, as the trail goes through the edge of the Rocky Mountain National Park and enters the Indian Peaks Wilderness. Big Rock Campground is a large site, strangely empty and eerie when I was there on 10 September as on that day the water had been turned off and everyone had departed, the summer season being at an end.

Due to the proximity of the cities of Denver and Boulder, the Indian Peaks Wilderness is very popular and, unlike many wilderness not to get any snow in the tent, I felt quite chilled. Luckily setting up camp soon becomes an automatic procedure on any walk and can be done in almost any conditions. Only after I'd donned my dry shirt and insulated jacket, slid into my down sleeping bag, fired up the stove and had some hot soup and coffee did I start to warm up. I had been right to stop.

As I lay in my sleeping bag listening to the wind roaring in the trees and the soft sigh of snow sliding down the tent flysheet, I thought I could hear someone shouting, an impression strong enough to have me looking out of the door a couple of times. All I could see were swirls of snow and I wasn't convinced enough I'd heard cries to venture out into the blizzard so, feeling a little puzzled, I stayed in the warmth of the tent. After several hours, the storm started to abate so, feeling bored and restless in the confines of my tiny nylon shelter, I ventured outside to have a look at the view. To the south where the pass lay, the peaks were still hidden in thick mist, but to the north the jagged ridge running from Mount Achonee to Navajo Peak stood out, clear and spectacular, with the last edges of the storm clouds drifting over its fresh, snow-spattered pinnacles. As I was taking in the magnificent scene I heard a dog bark and turned to see a distant figure with two dogs coming towards me. I had indeed heard shouting. The hiker had come over Arapaho Pass in the storm hoping to meet his brother, who was doing a three-day, high level cross-country trek along the Divide itself, at the pass to resupply him with food. Because of the storm he'd dropped down into the cirque where he thought his brother might be camping. I'd heard him wandering around in the storm calling out in case his brother, called Joel, was there. After chatting to me for a few minutes he set off back over the pass where he said he'd leave the food bag for his brother to collect. I said I'd look out for Joel and tell him where his food was if he turned up. Soon after

he departed, steady rain began to fall and I retreated to the tent.

Again the rain turned to snow and I woke to find several inches had fallen. However, patches of blue sky showed through the racing clouds and I'd soon packed the frozen tent and was heading up the steady climb to Arapaho Pass. The wind at the pass was bitterly cold but the view made up for it with the Front Range spread out to the south and the pink haze of the great plains fading away to the east. Ahead lay jagged rock ridges, tarn-filled cirques, grove-dotted meadows and forest-filled canyons. Above was a clearing sky. A black plastic garbage bag with Joel's supplies in it lay forlornly next to a boulder. There was no sign of anyone approaching.

From the pass the route drops towards the valley of the North Fork of Middle Boulder Creek, past the remnants of the Fourth of July Mine. After 2 miles (3.2km) and 1,200ft (360m) of descent a trail junction is reached where our route takes the Diamond Lake Trail. After a brief dip into the forest, this marvellous traversing trail climbs up to the alpine cirques containing Diamond Lake and Devil's Thumb Lake and then reaches Devil's Thumb Pass, from where there is another excellent view of the peaks to the south. I noted that although the lower snow had quickly burnt off in the now hot sun, it was lingering higher up. With several peaks to climb in the days ahead, this left me with the slight worry at the back of my mind that the snow might force me down to lower ground.

South of Devil's Thumb Pass the Front Range becomes a single crest rather than a complex of peaks and ridges. For the next few miles, this crest is followed above deep canyons and steep-sided, tarn-filled cirques, at first on a trail running just below the top and then along the undulating ridge itself, actually on the Continental Divide. The highest point reached is at 12,000ft (3,600m). Although the trail is faint, many large cairns mark the route. Eleven miles (17.6km) from Arapaho Pass, a gravel road, passable by car, is reached at Rollins Pass (11,700ft/3,510m). Here the beautiful Indian Peaks Wilderness is sadly left behind. An old jeep road, closed to traffic, leads south back to the Divide. There is no trail along the ridge but the going is easy. Dominating the view ahead is the great wedge of James Peak (13,294ft/ 3,988m) over which the route goes. As I approached this mountain along the narrow rocky ridge, I was a little perturbed at the apparent steepness and the covering of snow, although I was aware that the view was fore-shortened. Bits of jeep road and an abandoned aqueduct are followed before Rogers Pass (11,850ft/3,555m) is reached. Here starts the Ute Trail which is taken for a mile before being abandoned for the direct climb up James Peak.

Just after leaving the trail a tinge of green on the rough stony slopes reveals the presence of a tiny creek. Nearby there is a very small area of flat ground just big enough for a tent. In 1985 there was a small stone wall round it. In good weather this is a magnificent high level campsite at an altitude of 12,500ft (3,750m). However, it is very exposed and the stony ground does not take tent pegs easily so I would not recommend using it in stormy weather. Nor is there room for a big tent. I found I could barely squeeze my small one/two person model into the space between the walls and I was very glad there was no wind as I struggled to hammer the pegs a few inches into the rocky soil. The view from the site is wide-ranging and dramatic on three sides with the huge north shoulder of James Peak blocking the view to the south. Northwards, the long line of the Front Ranges stretches back into the Indian Peaks Wilder-ness, beyond which lies the tangle of peaks in Rocky Mountain National Park and the Never Summer Wilderness. To either side the subsidiary ridges, deep cirques between them, drop away steeply into the dark green valleys far below.

The clear evening sky turned gold at sunset as black shadows crept up the valleys, throwing into sharp relief the ridges and cirque walls. I took many photographs and sat outside the tent for hours in the gathering cold and darkness with the stove set up on a flat rock to boil water for coffee and soup to keep me warm. As the first stars appeared they were mirrored below by pinpricks of light in the valley, some moving, some fixed. The largest glow to the east was the town of Boulder. When I finally crawled into my tent, the flysheet was crisp with frost.

At 6.30am on the slopes of James Peak the temperature was −1°C (30°F). The valleys below were white with mist, while the hills to the south slowly turned gold in the rays of the rising sun. Two hours later with the tempera-ture now 3°C (38°F) I was on my way up James Peak. The route is simple, straight up the broad slopes to the top. Although steep it is not difficult, even when spattered with remnants of snow as on my ascent. It took me forty minutes to climb the half mile (0.8km) and 800ft (240m) to the flat summit and an extensive panorama of the Colorado Rockies. There is a register at the summit cairn. From the top there begins a marvellous 6 mile (9.6km) ridge walk over four more 13,000ft (3,900m) high peaks that never drops below 12,450ft (3735m) and provides a constant succession of changing views of the waves of mountains stretching north, west and south while to the east can be seen the great expanse of plains disappearing into the horizon, a reminder that the moun-tains do not go on for ever. Most of the way there is no trail but the terrain is ideal for cross-country travel, resembling in many ways a ridge walk in the British hills like the Mamores traverse. Only in storms should there be any problems, apart from one short scramble in the notch above Ice Lake, a mile beyond and 700ft (210m) below James Peak, where a rocky knoll has to be crossed or by-passed. With the rocks wet and slippery with melting snow, I took the

latter option and circumvented it via scree and talus slopes on the west side.

After the knoll, a steep climb leads to Mount Bancroft (which can be avoided by a contour under the summit talus slopes) and then, after a short descent, Parry Peak (13,391ft/4,017.3m) is ascended. The fine, neat summit of the latter, the highest point on the walk, is soon reached. Again there is a register. The view here shows that the Rockies are now reduced to just this single ridge, while to the north and south there are many parallel ranges giving breadth as well as length to the mountain chain. As I continued the walk from here I felt that I was moving from one area to another as I followed this ridge from the Indian Peaks Wilderness in the north, towards the rugged mass of the Gore Range which I could see rippling across the horizon to the south.

From Parry Peak, like James Peak named for a pioneer naturalist, the high level walk continues over Mounts Eva and Flora (13,130ft (3,939m) and 13,132ft (3,939.6m) high respectively), before the final descent of this section on jeep tracks to the ski slopes of Berthoud Pass at 11,300ft (3,390m). Here will be found the US40 highway and a ski lodge with café and gift shop. Grand Lake lies 52 miles (83.2km) to the north and the walk can be terminated here if your time has run out or the weather is stormy. The café was closed between the summer and ski seasons on my visit. I supped a few Cokes from a drinks machine and then left the pass and the cars to climb up under the ski lifts to the ridge above the pass and the start of another high level, cross-country walk along the Continental Divide on the crest of the Front Range.

*Looking north over the camp on the shoulder of James Peak.*

This is a very strenuous section with 6,300ft (1,890m) of ascent to cover in the next 20 miles (32km). I had no intention of starting this on the same day that I'd walked from James Peak. I just wanted to find a campsite away from the intrusion of civilization encountered at Berthoud Pass. However it was over 4 miles (6.4km) on from the pass that I finally found a good site. In between I followed the undulating ridge for a couple of miles on a good trail before traversing below Stanley Mountain, then descending to the deep notch of Vasquez Pass at 11,700ft (3,510m). Jim Wolf says in his *Guide to the Continental Divide Trail: Northern Colorado* that if you angle down to the pass too soon 'you will run into a steep and hazardous rockfall'. I can confirm this as, despite having his guidebook with me, that's exactly what I did. The crossing of this loose talus and scree

*View south from summit of James Peak.*

33

*Camp near Vasquez Pass.*

was difficult and nasty and I would advise staying high until immediately above the pass and then dropping down steeply into it.

From the pass a bit of the trail runs at timberline round to a grassy basin below the Divide in which can be found the headwaters of Vasquez Creek. Here, near the trickling stream, I camped on the first good site I had found on the route since the northern flanks of James Peak, 14½ miles (23.2km) and 4,750ft (1,425m) of ascent behind. Around the 11,550ft (3,465m) high site are stunted spruces and there is a good view out along the Vasquez valley to the northern Front Range peaks and the distant Never Summer range. I'd had a fine day for the high level walk, but, during the late afternoon, cirrus and then cumulus clouds drifted across the sky and blotted out the higher peaks. However, dawn arrived clear with a cold wind.

From the basin the route climbs steep, grassy slopes back to the Divide and then along a ridge to Vasquez Peak at 12,947ft (3,884m). Another undulating above timberline scenic walk over tundra-like terrain then ensues for 4 miles (6.4km) to Jones Pass at 12,450ft (3,735m). There are superb views from here, especially of the Gore Range, not far away to the south. Below many of the cols are more basins, several with small lakes, where camps could be set up.

At Jones Pass our route leaves the Continental Divide and heads for the Gore Range. Although departing from the Front Range, this last 22 miles (35.2km) is a scenic and fitting finish to the walk and provides the convenience of ending in the town of Silverthorne on Interstate 70 from where buses can be caught. The final section starts with a bone-shaking, knee-jarring, steep descent of over 2,000ft (600m) down a jeep road from Jones Pass to the beautiful Bobtail Creek valley whose luxurious groves and rich meadows are a pleasant sight after the rugged scenery of the high level ridges. A good pack trail ascends the valley over which tower the massive walls of Pettingell Peak and Hagar Mountain. There are many possible campsites near Bobtail Creek. After 2½ miles (4km) the trail climbs above timberline up the west wall of the valley in a series of switchbacks, before contouring above green cirques and the forested canyon of the South Fork of Williams Fork into which it eventually descends. Campsites abound in the valley. A popular local walk is a 29-mile (46.4-km) circuit of the hills above the South Fork known as The Loop and as I descended I met two backpackers setting out on this trek.

The valley bottom would seem a good place to stop after the walk from near Berthoud Pass and there are plenty of possible campsites but I was enjoying the fine day so much that I continued, following the creek downstream to a trail junction. Here the route takes the lefthand trail signposted Ptarmigan Pass. The steep trail is blazed and cairned as it climbs 1,500ft (450m) to the 11,777ft (3,533m) timberline pass. I camped just below the pass on the north side by a tiny creeklet, another scenic site. The evening began clear, but by dusk rain was falling and I was glad I'd pushed on and made the most of the good weather. Dawn brought clouds and a smattering of new snow on the flanks of Hagar Mountain. A traverse of open hillsides on the far side of the pass, by a mixture of pack trail, jeep road and cross-country, gives good views of the Gore Range, now just a few miles away, before the long, forested descent to Silverthorne is undertaken. The final few miles into Silverthorne are on private roads – contact the Forest Service before the trek for the current access position.

Silverthorne is a sizeable town offering motels, restaurants and all other services, a good place to relax and unwind from the walk and to reflect on the solitude and mountain grandeur to be found only a few miles away along the Front Range. Then you can start the journey back home, your mind full of plans for your next mountain trek.

## THE ROUTE

| MILEAGE/(KM) | | PLACE | ELEVATION | |
| --- | --- | --- | --- | --- |
| | | | ft | m |
| 0.0 | 0.0 | Grand Lake | 8,400 | 2,520 |
| 7.7 | 12.3 | Colorado River Campsite | 8,300 | 2,490 |
| 13.8 | 22.0 | Big Rock Campground | 8,350 | 2,505 |
| 23.5 | 37.6 | Arapaho Creek | 10,650 | 3,195 |
| 24.3 | 38.8 | Caribou Lake | 11,150 | 3,345 |
| 25.2 | 40.3 | Arapaho Pass | 11,900 | 3,570 |
| 28.8 | 46.0 | Diamond Lake | 10,950 | 3,285 |
| 32.6 | 52.1 | Devil's Thumb Lake | 11,150 | 3,345 |
| 36.4 | 58.2 | Rollins Pass | 11,700 | 3,510 |
| 41.8 | 66.8 | Rogers Pass | 11,850 | 3,555 |
| 43.4 | 69.4 | James Peak | 13,294 | 3,988.2 |
| 46.2 | 73.9 | Parry Peak | 13,391 | 4,017.3 |
| 47.3 | 75.6 | Mount Eva | 13,130 | 3,939 |
| 49.5 | 79.2 | Mount Flora | 13,132 | 3,939.6 |
| 52.1 | 83.3 | Berthoud Pass | 11,300 | 3,390 |
| 56.4 | 90.2 | Vasquez Pass | 11,700 | 3,510 |
| 59.1 | 94.5 | Vasquez Peak | 12,947 | 3,884.1 |
| 63.3 | 101.2 | Jones Pass | 12,450 | 3,735 |
| 66.1 | 105.7 | Bobtail Valley | 10,400 | 3,120 |
| 74.2 | 118.7 | South Fork, Williams Fork | 10,350 | 3,105 |
| 77.0 | 123.2 | Ptarmigan Pass | 11,777 | 3,533.1 |
| 85.0 | 136.0 | Silverthorne | 8,750 | 2,625 |

*Campsite in Vasquez Creek basin.*

From the resort of **Grand Lake** (8,400ft, Mile 0), take the trail along the shore of Shadow Mountain Lake entering Rocky Mountain National Park (Mile 2). The route continues along and above the lake, crossing a number of creeks before reaching the Colorado River, here just a stream (Mile 5), and then the Columbine Bay Campsite (Mile 6) and, just after leaving the national park, the **Colorado River Campsite** (8,300ft, Mile 7.7) in the Arapaho National Recreation Area. The trail then crosses wooded Knight Ridge via a couple of switchbacks and descends to Lake Granby, the shore of which is

followed to a roadhead (Mile 12.8) Take the gravel road past Roaring Fork, Moraine and **Big Rock Campgrounds** (8,350ft, Mile 13.8) and along the shore of Monarch Lake. Beyond the lake, the route enters the Indian Peaks Wilderness and the road soon becomes a pack trail which is then left for the signed Arapaho Trail (8,400ft, Mile 16.2); this takes the walker across bridged Buchanan Creek and then switchbacks up a steep ascent above **Arapaho Creek**, which is finally forded (9,750ft, Mile 21.7) just after a good campsite is passed. Further switchbacks lead through the meadows of

Coyote Park to the alpine basin containing **Caribou Lake** (11,150ft, Mile 24.3). The climb continues out of the cirque to **Arapaho Pass** (11,900ft, Mile 25.2) where there is a trail junction. The Arapaho Trail turns left and descends to a junction with the wide Diamond Lake Trail (10,500ft, Mile 27.6) which is followed for just over a mile to another junction where the left fork is taken (**Diamond Lake** lies just up the right fork) on an undulating traverse to a signed junction (10,700ft, Mile 31) where the Devil's Thumb Trail is taken. This leads past Jasper Lake to **Devil's Thumb Lake** (11,150ft, Mile 32.6). From here, a pack trail leads up to the Continental Divide (12,000ft, Mile 33.6), from where large cairns lead for ¼ mile to the Corona Trail which is followed to the gravel road at **Rollins Pass** (11,700ft, Mile 36.4). The road is taken southwards for ½ mile and then left for jeep tracks which lead back to the Divide, which is then followed cross-country until a jeep road is joined on the west side of the ridge (11,850ft, Mile 39.4) and taken for 2 miles before an abandoned aqueduct leads ¼ mile to **Rogers Pass** (11,850ft, Mile 41.8). From the pass, take the Ute Trail for a mile on to the broad north shoulder of **James Peak** which is climbed directly to the summit (13,294ft, Mile 43.4). The next 6 miles consists of a cross-country high level traverse of **Parry Peak** and **Mounts Eva** and **Flora**. The only tricky section is at the notch above Ice Lake (12,600ft, Mile 44.4), where a bit of easy scrambling is required. From **Mount Flora** (13,132ft, Mile 49.5), a descent leads down to jeep tracks, ski slopes and the highway at **Berthoud Pass** (11,300ft, Mile 52.1). A ski service road leads out of the resort for a mile to a trail which climbs for another mile to an unnamed 12,391ft peak. An undulating walk on sketchy trails then leads along the Divide to a steep descent to **Vasquez Pass** (11,700ft, Mile 56.4). Leave the Divide to traverse on its north side for ½ mile beyond the pass to pick up a jeep trail and then a foot trail which is followed to Vasquez Creek (11,550ft, Mile 57.4). A steep cross-country climb leads back to the Divide and **Vasquez Peak** (12,947ft, Mile 59.1). The ridge is then followed, at first cross-country, but then on pack trail to the gravel road at **Jones Pass** (12,450ft, Mile 63.3). From the pass, a steep descent on a jeep road leads to **Bobtail Creek** (10,400ft, Mile 66.1), which is followed upstream on jeep and pack trails for 2½ miles before taking a switchbacking trail up to a narrow ridge (12,300ft, Mile 69.8). An undulating route above Steelman Creek is then followed over a number of minor tops to a pass (11,750ft, Mile 72.5), from where the route descends to pick up a trail at the forest edge, continuing down to the **South Fork of Williams Fork** (10,350ft, Mile 74). Half a mile downstream the **Ptarmigan Pass Trail** is taken up to the pass itself (11,771ft, Mile 77).

A complex route then leads on an undulating descent via jeep and pack trails down to the town of **Silverthorne** (8,750ft, Mile 85). Check with the Forest Service for current access details before undertaking this last section as the roads into the town are private.

## MAPS

USGS 1:24,000 topographic maps: Grand Lake; Shadow Mountain; Strawberry Lake; Monarch Lake; East Portal; Empire; Berthoud Pass; Byers Peak; Loveland Pass; Dillon.

## RECOMMENDED GUIDEBOOK

*Guide to the Continental Divide Trail: Northern Colorado* by James R. Wolf (Continental Divide Trail Society).

# The Bridger Wilderness and Wind River Range:
## Lower Green Lake to South Pass
## 118 miles (189km)

*When traces of blood begin to mark your trail you'll see something, maybe.*

Edward Abbey   *Desert Solitaire*

A long line of granite peaks runs south-east into central Wyoming from the mass of mountains in the north of the state to terminate abruptly, high above a desert plateau. These mountains make up the Wind River Range, the last segment of the Rocky Mountains before the range is split by the Great Divide Basin, so called because here the watershed of the continent splits in two, water that runs into the basin disappearing into its desert heart instead of heading for either the Pacific or Atlantic Oceans. The Wind Rivers are a high, heavily glaciated, alpine range of spectacular peaks, reaching 13,804ft (4,141m) on Gannett Peak, the highest in Wyoming, and containing seven of the ten largest glaciers in the USA outside Alaska. The Continental Divide runs along the crest of the range and along its western flank lies the 392,000-acre Bridger Wilderness, named for one of the most famous of the mountain men and fur trappers, Jim Bridger, who explored the area in the 1820s. On its east lies the 191,000-acre Fitzpatrick Wilderness Area, plus two primitive areas. These protected regions have an extensive and well-marked trail system.

The walk described here runs north-south through the Bridger Wilderness paralleling the main crest of the Wind River Range on trails via a high level route, although the above timberline terrain is so open that any number of variations, both cross-country and on trails, could be taken. The walk is 118 miles (189km) long and shouldn't take more than ten days (I did it in a week). However, your pack will be heavy at the start, as there are no supply points along the route although meals can be obtained at Big Sandy Lodge after 72 miles (115km) if you stay there. Snacks and candy can be obtained at South Pass City (which is not a town!) at the end of the walk. The area is very popular and certain regulations apply between 1 July and 10 September. These are that no groups should number more than ten people, no fires should be lit and tents should be more than 200ft (60m) from any lakeshore, unless they are hidden from view. There are no other restrictions on where you can camp. In fact, the wilderness authorities deliberately don't make any site recommendations in order to avoid overuse of any area. This approach is welcome as the area abounds in fine potential sites. Summer weather is usually good but snow may lie on high level trails until mid-July and start to fall again in September. Route finding should be no problem as the trails are well marked and the country is open. Only on the last sections of the descent to South Pass City which lie outside the Bridger Wilderness are you likely to encounter problems but if you lose the trail the direction in which to go is fairly

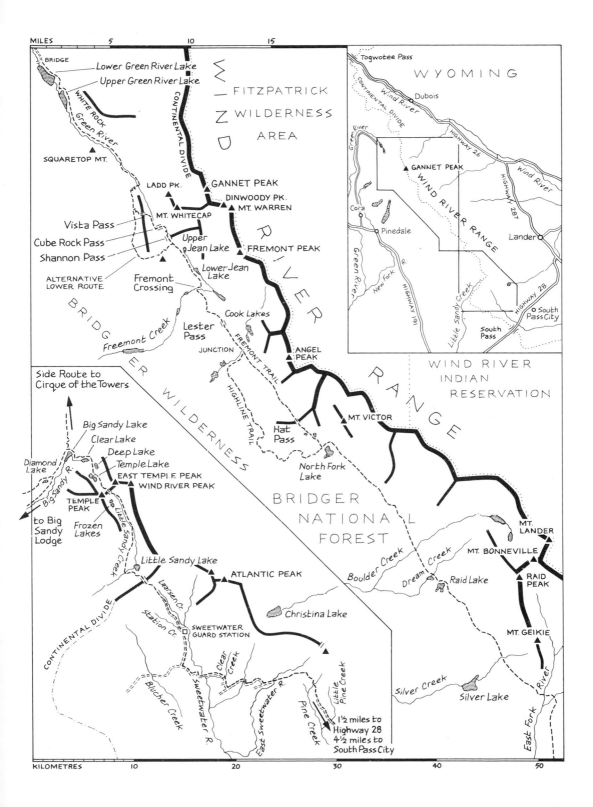

MILES    5         10         15

BRIDGE
Lower Green River Lake
Upper Green River Lake

WHITE ROCK
Green River

W I N D

FITZPATRICK

WILDERNESS

AREA

SQUARETOP MT.

CONTINENTAL DIVIDE

LADD PK.          GANNET PEAK
                  DINWOODY PK.
MT. WHITECAP      MT. WARREN

Vista Pass
Cube Rock Pass        Upper
Shannon Pass          Jean Lake        FREMONT PEAK

ALTERNATIVE                Lower Jean Lake
LOWER ROUTE      Fremont
                 Crossing

R   I   V   E   R

BRIDGER                           Cook Lakes

Freemont Creek   Lester
                 Pass
                 JUNCTION        FREMONT TRAIL        ANGEL
                                                      PEAK

Side Route to
Cirque of the Towers

WILDERNESS

HIGHLINE TRAIL

Hat
Pass

Big Sandy Lake
Clear Lake
Diamond        Deep Lake
Lake           Temple Lake
Big Sandy R.   EAST TEMPLE PEAK
               WIND RIVER PEAK        North Fork
TEMPLE                                Lake
PEAK
Frozen                       BRIDGER
Lakes
to Big                       NATIONAL
Sandy            Little Sandy Creek
Lodge          Little Sandy Lake          FOREST
                            ATLANTIC PEAK

CONTINENTAL DIVIDE

MT. VICTOR

R   A   N   G   E

MT.
LANDER
MT. BONNEVILLE
Boulder Creek    Dream Creek    Raid Lake    RAID
                                             PEAK

Larsen Cr.
Station Cr.        SWEETWATER
                   GUARD STATION        Christina Lake
Blucher Creek      Clear Creek
                   Sweetwater R.
                   East Sweetwater R.
                   Pine Creek
                   Little Pine Creek
                   1½ miles to
                   Highway 28
                   4½ miles to
                   South Pass City

MT. GEIKIE

Silver Creek        Silver Lake

East Fork River

**WYOMING inset:**

Togwotee Pass
WYOMING
Wind River       Dubois
CONTINENTAL DIVIDE
HIGHWAY 26
Green River
GANNET PEAK
WIND RIVER RANGE
Cora
Pinedale                          Lander
HIGHWAY 287
Wind River
HIGHWAY 191
New Fork R.
Green River
Little Sandy Creek
HIGHWAY 28
South       South Pass City
Pass
South Pass

WIND RIVER
INDIAN
RESERVATION

KILOMETRES    10              20              30              40              50

*(Preceding pages) Camp in Vista Pass.*

obvious and bushwhacking is easy (as I found out!).

The route begins at the foot of Lower Green River Lake at the end of a gravel access road 40 miles (64km) from the town of Cora. The start is along the Highline Trail which will be followed for much of the journey. This runs here along the eastern shores of Lower and Upper Green River Lakes, soon entering the Bridger Wilderness. I set off along this trail on a fine day impressed by the imposing mountains ahead of me, especially the huge block of rock that is Squaretop Mountain (11,695ft/ 3,508.5m) and which grows in size and dominance as the walker approaches, before disappearing as you pass below its sheer walls. Gradually the steep-sided peaks draw the walker in as the lakes are left behind and the narrow, forested Green River valley is entered and a passage threaded between Squaretop Mountain and White Rock, the mountain wall to the east. After crossing the meadows of Beaver and Three Forks Parks and fording the Green River on a two pole bridge, I followed switchbacks away from the river and up to Trail Creek Park and a trail junction. Here a decision has to be made. I consulted my maps and decided to go for a high level route via Vista and Shannon Passes. The alternative, which is probably a good idea in bad weather or early in the season, is to stay on the Highline Trail, a slightly longer, but lower and more sheltered route. This is the route described in Jim Wolf's *Guide to the Continental Divide Trail: Wyoming* which I was carrying.

I finished my first day by camping in 10,120ft (3,036m) Vista Pass itself, where there is a small pool from which to draw water and a superb view that explains the name of the pass across the Green River canyon to Ladd Peak (12,957ft/3,887m), Mount Whitecap

(13,020ft/3,906m), Sulphur Peak (12,825ft/ 3,847.5m) and Stroud Peak (12,198ft/ 3,659.4m). The wide pass is just on timberline, line, the flat ground dotted with wind-stunted whitebark pine and Engelmann's spruce. I was there in early August and mosquitos were prevalent despite a gusty wind and some black clouds that poured in from the west. August also means people and I'd met forty or so during this 15-mile (24-km) day, thirty-six of them backpackers descending from the high country. I was to meet around the same number every day throughout the walk except for the last section outside the Bridger Wilderness, but I always had campsites to myself.

The dark clouds of the first evening gave way

*Bridger Wilderness sign.*

to heavy rain during the night and an overcast dawn. I could see faint traces of fresh snow on those peaks that were visible. The pond on Vista Pass was black under the steely sky and the granite cliffs cold and grey. For the 3 miles (4.8km) to 11,200ft (3,360m) Shannon Pass the walker is in a sterile world of rock, seeming unfriendly and threatening in the weather conditions that I had. However, the final long climb up to the pass through a narrow boulder-filled ravine gave good views back to the Green River and Squaretop Mountain. Soon after the pass, the Highline Trail comes in from the west and the route reaches the large Upper Jean Lake. Here I met a party of eight boy scouts with two leaders who I talked to for a while. They thought I was a rock climber, not a backpacker, because of my internal frame pack. They all had heavily loaded pack frames. I was to meet two more groups of eight scouts during the day. While I was talking to the first group light snow started to fall, but soon afterwards the weather began to clear.

Rows of jagged peaks line the trail all the way to Lester Pass (11,100ft/3,330m) 8 miles (12.8km) from the two Jean Lakes, after which the country becomes flatter and more open with the mountains farther away and more widely spaced. Once across the pass the trail dips into the trees briefly and arrives at Cook Lakes. Shortly beyond the lakes, which are many and large, I left the Highline Trail and the guidebook route again to take the higher Fremont Trail and climb up to the lake-dotted, mountain-rimmed and spacious Bald Mountain Basin from where there is an impressive view of Angel Peak at 12,402ft (3,720.6km). At the head of the basin, I crossed an unnamed 10,800ft (3,240m) pass that gave a great view back north to the cluster of spires and glaciers along the Divide and around Titcomb Basin, a popular backcountry destination, made especially memorable by the appearance of the sun. Camp that night was a little down from

*A rattlesnake.*

the pass at 10,550ft (3,165m) just on timberline by some stunted whitebark pine, with a tiny trickle of a creek for water. The terrain here is such that there are myriad prospective sites that can be found wherever and whenever you want to stop.

Mostly open country continues up to obvious but gentle 10,848ft (3,254.4m) Hat Pass which I scurried over in a bitter wind (there was ice on the shallow pools here), to the sanctuary of a sheltered forest and lake descent (during which I saw an elk) that leads to North Fork Lake and the rejoining of the guidebook route. From here the trail is marked as both the Fremont and the Highline Trail (on the map it's called the latter). Of this section I wrote in my journal 'pretty country but the wind kept me moving'. The trail runs in an almost straight line here, south-east across a shelf spread with clumps of trees, meadows and shallow lakes best described as a vast upland park. There are good views of the rugged spires of Mount Bonneville (12,570ft/3,771m) and surrounding peaks, and across Sheep Creek you catch a first glimpse of the west side of the famous Cirque of the Towers, a major climbing area. Near Raid Lake a herd of wild sheep watched me from the nearby slopes. Again I could pick a camp site just about wherever I

Hat Pass.

Backpackers on the Little Sandy Lake Trail.

wanted and the one I chose was on a grassy shelf just above the North Fork Silver Creek below Mount Geikie (12,378ft/3,713.4m). A warm appearing sunset belied the still cold wind. I watched it from the shelter of the tent. Coyotes howling nearby woke me in the night, a wild sound redolent of the wilderness. By dawn the temperature was zero and there was frost on the tent. A thin crescent moon hung above the dark trees. Pink clouds sailed by high above as a thin, pink line spread out to the west. 'Cold and clear, white frost on the grass. Sun just touching land to the west. Everything sharp and distinct' I wrote in my journal.

Four hours and 13 miles (20.8km) of descent with good views of the canyon of the East River and the serrated Cirque of the Towers skyline took me out of the Bridger Wilderness and down a dirt road to Big Sandy Lodge (address Big Sandy Lodge, Post Office, Boulder, Wyom-

ing 82923) in time for lunch. Here I rented a cabin and booked in for three meals, which are only available to guests. There is a Forest Service Campground nearby but nowhere to resupply. The lodge and campground are 1½ miles (2.4km) off the route so you can save 3 miles (4.8km) of walking if you pass them by, but, if you want a shower and some real food, plus conversation with interesting people in an informal atmosphere, I'd go for the lodge.

Back on the route (at first signed the Diamond Lake Trail and then the Big Sandy Lake Trail) and back in the Bridger Wilderness, I headed for the final and most glorious flourish of this traverse of the Wind River Range. Once past Big Sandy Lake the Little Sandy Lake Trail is joined. (The left-hand fork leads in 3¼ miles (5.2km) over Big Sandy Pass to Lonesome Lake in the Cirque of the Towers, a recommended side trip if you have time. I wish I'd done it!) There were many other walkers around Big Sandy Lake and several tents pitched in the woods.

At Clear Lake a grim glacier-carved world of rock is entered with cirques, spires and peaks, snowpatches and small glaciers, cold mountain pools and sparkling creeks all around. Five people had still managed to find sites for their tents near the lake despite the barren terrain. As I ascended, I had close-up views of the soaring sheer rock walls and summits of Haystack Mountain (11,978ft/3,593.4m), East Temple Peak (12,590ft/3,777m) and Temple Peak (12,972ft/3,891.6m). The trail passes the dramatically – situated Deep and Temple Lakes before climbing to its high point at an unnamed 11,500ft (3,450m) pass between Temple and East Temple Peaks. Cairns mark the faint trail here. From the pass, the trail drops down to a lake at the head of the rock-lined, glacier-sliced canyon of Little Sandy Creek on the start of its descent out of the mountains. There is good scenery along the upper reaches of the creek, but all too soon the forest appears. To the south

I caught glimpses of the below timberline sagebrush and grassland plains of the Great Divide Basin. I stayed in the mountains for one more night, making camp in lodgepole pine forest just above where the trail crossed the fast and noisy Little Sandy Creek on a log.

The continuing descent through a mixture of forest and sagebrush leads out of the Bridger Wilderness and via jeep tracks into the foothills of the Wind River Range. Across Little Sandy Lake there are final views back to the high peaks before the last 10,000ft (3,000m) pass is crossed, the only one on the route that takes the walker across the Continental Divide. From here on the route is obscure, much of it being on unmaintained trail. I lost the trail at one point and had to bushwhack (not difficult) on a compass bearing before I found a jeep track that led to Pine Creek. The route described in the guidebook and the trails marked on my map did not coincide at this point. Here I set up camp on a pleasant, grassy spot by the boundary of the Bridger-Teton National Forest and next to a steep, boulder-strewn slope. A mule deer and a porcupine came out of the bushes to inspect the tent. Earlier in the day I'd seen another elk. The evening was clear so I just pitched the inner tent to keep the mosquitos off. During the night, rain began to fall so I had to slip out of my sleeping bag and erect the flysheet. By the creek a moose was grazing.

With just 6 miles (9.6km) to go I was in South Pass City by 10am. Along this last dirt road section there are views out across the sagebrush plains of the basin to the broad, almost imperceptible South Pass itself and several isolated desert mountains. Watch out here for rattlesnakes which can be found in the Great Divide Basin, especially if you venture off the tracks into the bushes. Once Highway 28 is reached the walk is effectively over but unless time is pressing I would recommend that you go the extra 3 miles (4.8km) on jeep tracks to South Pass City. This is not a town as such,

*Bill Lowe's store, South Pass City.*

but a state park and restored ghost town kept much as it was a hundred years ago and more. I found it fascinating to wander round the stores, hotels and houses and down the dusty high street and wonder what it must have been like to live in a town with no cars. I particularly noticed the lack of wires! The settlement appeared here due to a gold rush that occurred in the area in the 1860s when it and other local and now deserted towns such as Atlantic City were founded. South Pass itself was already well known, being the easiest wagon route across the Continental Divide for pioneers heading west having both an easy gradient and a guaranteed water supply. As such, South Pass became a focal point of westward expansion for first the Oregon Trail, then other routes, including the first Pony Express service, and the first Mormons heading for Utah.

Escaping from this area, unless you have someone coming to pick you up, could mean hitch-hiking or a long wait as there is just one bus a week along Highway 28, running between Lander to the east and Farson to the west, both 40 miles away. South Pass City has one café,

Bill Lowe's Carissa Exchange, where you can buy, according to my journal 'only coffee, soft drinks, ice-cream and hot dogs'. I drank gallons of Coca-Cola here. The Great Divide Basin is a lot hotter than the mountains! There is also a register of Continental Divide hikers who've passed through in the café, which makes interesting reading. In one of the 'stores' in the town there is a small post office to which you could send yourself packages (General Delivery, South Pass City, Wyoming 82520) if you want clean clothes or extra food before heading out. On Highway 28 there is a gas station which sells a few groceries (I bought a quart of white gas, a white sliced loaf, a ½lb butter, coffee and a tin of soup). Otherwise the area is empty, left to its memories of wagon trains straining over the pass, full of pioneers eager to see water that finished up in the Pacific rather than the Atlantic Ocean and would-be miners arriving, hoping to make a fortune by discovering gold in the creeks that tumble down from the Wind Rivers to lose themselves in the dust and sand of the Great Divide Basin.

*Lower Green River Lake and Squaretop Mountain.*

Deep Lake and East Temple Peak.

Main Street, South Pass City.

# THE ROUTE

| MILEAGE/(KM) | | PLACE | ELEVATION | |
| --- | --- | --- | --- | --- |
| | | | ft | m |
| 0.0 | 0.0 | Green River Bridge | 7,950 | 2,385 |
| 3.2 | 5.1 | Upper Green River Lake | 8,000 | 2,400 |
| 15.0 | 24.0 | Vista Pass | 10,120 | 3,036 |
| 18.0 | 28.8 | Shannon Pass | 11,120 | 3,336 |
| 20.0 | 32.0 | Upper Jean Lake | 10,799 | 3,239.7 |
| 23.0 | 36.8 | Fremont Crossing | 10,250 | 3,075 |
| 27.8 | 44.4 | Lester Pass | 11,100 | 3,330 |
| 30.4 | 48.6 | Fremont Trail junction | 10,250 | 3,075 |
| 38.4 | 61.4 | Hat Pass | 10,848 | 3,254.4 |
| 40.4 | 64.6 | North Fork Lake | 9,754 | 2,926.2 |
| 45.2 | 72.3 | Halls Creek | 9,800 | 2,940 |
| 48.5 | 77.6 | Dream Creek | 9,900 | 2,970 |
| 53.2 | 85.1 | Scab Creek Trail junction | 10,350 | 3,105 |
| 56.7 | 90.7 | East Fork River | 9,750 | 2,925 |
| 61.7 | 98.7 | Fish Creek | 9,800 | 2,940 |
| 69.9 | 111.8 | Diamond Lake Trail junction | 9,300 | 2,790 |
| 71.9 | 115.0 | Diamond Lake | 9,500 | 2,850 |
| 73.9 | 118.2 | Big Sandy Lake | 9,700 | 2,910 |
| 76.0 | 121.6 | Clear Lake | 10,000 | 3,000 |
| 77.5 | 124.0 | Deep Lake | 10,500 | 3,150 |
| 78.6 | 125.7 | Temple Lake | 10,650 | 3,195 |
| 79.8 | 127.6 | Unnamed pass | 11,500 | 3,450 |
| 80.8 | 129.2 | Little Sandy Creek | 10,600 | 3,180 |
| 90.0 | 144.0 | Larsen Creek | 9,200 | 2,760 |
| 92.7 | 148.3 | Lowline Trail junction | 8,600 | 2,580 |
| 93.6 | 149.7 | Station Creek | 8,300 | 2,490 |
| 98.0 | 156.8 | Sweetwater River | 7,850 | 2,355 |
| 99.4 | 159.0 | Clear Creek | 8,100 | 2,430 |
| 102.3 | 163.6 | Little Sweetwater River | 8,100 | 2,430 |
| 104.0 | 166.4 | East Sweetwater Valley | 8,300 | 2,490 |
| 109.5 | 175.2 | Pine Creek | 9,100 | 2,730 |
| 114.5 | 183.2 | Dead Ox Creek | 8,150 | 2,445 |
| 114.9 | 183.8 | Wyoming Highway 28 | 8,150 | 2,445 |
| 118.0 | 188.8 | South Pass City | 7,950 | 2,385 |

The walk starts at a bridge over the **Green River** (7,950ft Mile 0) at the end of a gravel wilderness access road, 40 miles from the little hamlet of Cora. The trail, signed the Highline Trail runs along the east shores of **Lower** and **Upper Green River Lakes**, entering the Bridger Wilderness after ¼ mile, towards the huge bulk of Squaretop Mountain. Beyond the lakes, continue alongside the Green River into a narrow, wooded gorge to a trail junction (9,600ft, Mile 14.3) where the Shannon Pass Trail is taken to **Vista Pass** (10,120ft, Mile 15) where open country is entered and up through Cube Rock Pass to **Shannon Pass** (11,120ft, Mile 18). Three-quarters of a mile beyond the pass, the Highline Trail is rejoined as it comes in from the right and the combined trail descends to **Upper** and **Lower Jean Lakes** and then **Fremont Crossing** (10,250ft, Mile 23). A steady, but easy ascent then leads to **Lester Pass** (11,100ft, Mile 27.8) and a descent back into forest and a **trail junction** (10,250ft, Mile 30.4), where the Highline Trail is left for the Fremont Trail. This trail climbs to an unnamed 10,850ft pass, then undulates above timberline to the gentle but obvious **Hat Pass** (10,848ft, Mile 38.4) from where it drops back down into the forest and passes a series of small lakes before arriving at large **North Fork Lake** (9,754ft, Mile 40.4) where the Highline Trail is joined again. From here to the junction with the Diamond Lake Trail in 29½ miles the names Fremont and Highline appear interchangeably for the name of the trail. Through this section the trail runs in almost a straight line in a south-easterly direction along a plateau on the south-west edge of the high peaks of the Wind River Range, past a series of small lakes. For the 8½ miles to **Dream Creek** (9,900ft, Mile 48.5) the route is mostly in forest but it's then in open country for 8 more miles to the **East Fork River** (9,750ft, Mile 56.7) After a short ascent, the trail beyond the river turns away a little from the main peaks and descends slowly past **Fish Creek** (9,800ft, Mile 61.7) to the **Diamond Lake Trail junction** (9,300ft, Mile 69.9). Big Sandy Lodge and Campground lie 1½ miles south of this junction. Our route turns north-eastwards and ascends slowly past **Diamond Lake** to **Big Sandy Lake** (9,700ft, Mile 73.9). At a junction on the lakeshore, the route turns south-eastwards again along the Little Sandy Lake Trail climbing through rocky terrain past **Clear**, **Deep** and **Temple Lakes** to a high **unnamed pass** (11,500ft, Mile 79.8) between Temple and East Temple Peaks. From Deep Lake the trail is sketchy, but there are cairns and the general line of the route is obvious. A steep descent leads to a lake at the head of the long canyon of **Little Sandy Creek**. Four and a half miles down this valley leave its floor at a stone marker (keep a sharp eye out for this). From here the trail traverses above the creek before dropping down to cross it near Little Sandy Lake,

then crossing the Continental Divide by an unnamed pass and dropping down to **Larsen Creek** (9,200ft, Mile 90). Half a mile further on, the Bridger Wilderness is left, then after almost a mile more a roadhead is reached. Two miles down the jeep road is another road junction by **Station Creek** (8,300ft, Mile 93.6) where the road heading south is followed to the Sweetwater River (7,850ft, Mile 98). Still on a jeep road the route runs beside Clear Creek then over a hilltop and ridge to the **Little Sweetwater River** (8,100ft, Mile 102.3) and over another crest to the **East Sweetwater Valley** (8,300ft, Mile 104). Jeep tracks are now taken for ½ mile mile to the start of the Sweetwater Trail which has faint tread but is marked by blazes and which is followed for 3½ miles to the more clearly defined Pine Creek Trail. This trail leads to a crossing of **Pine Creek** (9,100ft, Mile 109.5) and then, after crossing a number of low rises, a faint jeep road which is followed to Little Pine Creek and then **Dead Ox Creek** (8,150ft Mile 114.9) and ½ mile further **Wyoming Highway 28**. It's then just 3 more miles to **South Pass City** (7,950ft, Mile 118).

## MAPS

USGS 1:24,000 topographic maps: Green River Lakes; Squaretop Mountain; Gannett Peak; Bridger Lakes; Fremont Peak South; Horseshoe Lake; Mt Bonneville (1:625000); Big Sandy Opening; Temple Peak; Sweetwater Gap; Jensen Meadows; Sweetwater Needles; Christina Lake; Anderson Ridge; South Pass City.

## RECOMMENDED GUIDEBOOK

*Guide to the Continental Divide Trail: Wyoming* by Jim Wolf (Continental Divide Trail Society). Note, though, that in two places the trail as described here takes a higher route than that described in this guidebook.

# The Volcanic Wildernesses of the Oregon Cascades:
## Williamette Pass to the Columbia River
## 238 miles (381km)

*There is an energy generated by great mountains that is unlike any other force in nature. Something magical happens up there.*

Cindy Ross  *Journey on the Crest*

Seven hundred miles (1,120km) long, the Cascade Mountain Range runs all the way from northern California to Canada through the states of Oregon and Washington. The chain is not continuous, being split by the deep trench of the Columbia River valley, and the resulting sections are very different from each other. The Volcanic Wildernesses trek, the first of three walks in the Cascades described in this book, is situated in the rolling terrain of northern Oregon. Here the Cascades consist mainly of gentle, forested hills interspersed with a series of placid lakes, pleasant for walking in, but hardly spectacular or exciting. However, totally at variance with the general feel of the area is the line of huge volcanoes that stretches in total from Lassen Peak in northern California to Mount Garibaldi in south-west British Columbia and which gives the Cascades a very distinct character. These volcanoes are not dead either, as was shown in 1980 when Mount St Helens in southern Washington erupted violently after being dormant for 123 years. Steam and ash were sent 10,000ft (3,000m) into the air above the mountain. The greatest

concentration of ice-carved, volcanic peaks, although not the highest individual summits, occurs in northern Oregon and it is through this area that our walk goes, linking together the series of wilderness areas set up to protect these magnificent mountains. In this region, the volcanic peaks are in the 10–11,000ft (3,000–3,300m) elevation range, with Mount Hood the highest at 11,235ft (3,370.5m). Rising 4–5,000ft (1,200–1,500m) above the surrounding terrain the rugged volcanoes, their red and black rock and scree slopes splashed white with glaciers, tower over the forest and can be seen from many miles away.

Starting in the south in the Three Sisters Wilderness, the walk runs for 237 miles (379.2km) through the Mount Washington, Mount Jefferson and Mount Hood Wildernesses before descending via the spectacular Eagle Creek Trail to the Columbia River on the border with Washington. The route is basically that of the Pacific Crest Trail (PCT) although some sections are marked as being the Oregon Skyline Trail which the PCT has replaced, and near the end it leaves the PCT for the Eagle Creek Trail. This is a walk of contrasts with some sections in deep forest and others on barren volcanic cinders. Despite the varying

*(Opposite) Tunnel Falls, Eagle Creek Trail.*

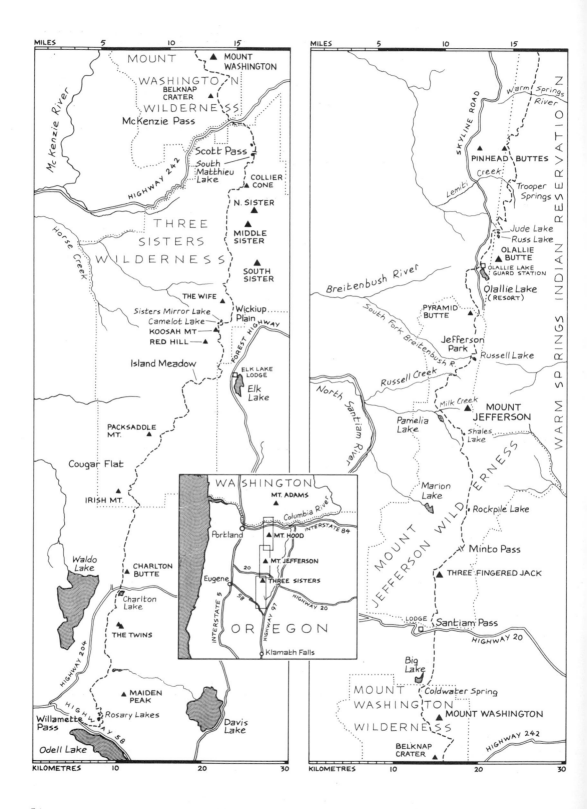

MILES 5 10 15

MOUNT
WASHINGTON
WILDERNESS
McKenzie Pass
McKenzie River
▲ MOUNT WASHINGTON
BELKNAP CRATER ▲

Scott Pass
South Matthieu Lake
COLLIER CONE ▲

N. SISTER ▲

THREE SISTERS WILDERNESS
MIDDLE SISTER ▲

SOUTH SISTER ▲

Horse Creek
THE WIFE ▲
Sisters Mirror Lake
Camelot Lake
KOOSAH MT ▲
RED HILL ▲
Wickiup Plain

HIGHWAY 242
FOREST HIGHWAY

Island Meadow
ELK LAKE LODGE
Elk Lake

PACKSADDLE MT. ▲

Cougar Flat

IRISH MT. ▲

WASHINGTON
MT. ADAMS ▲
Columbia River
Portland
INTERSTATE 84
MT. HOOD ▲
20
MT. JEFFERSON ▲
Eugene
58
THREE SISTERS ▲
HIGHWAY 20
INTERSTATE 5
HIGHWAY 97
OREGON
Klamath Falls

Waldo Lake
CHARLTON BUTTE ▲
Charlton Lake

THE TWINS ▲
HIGHWAY 204

MAIDEN PEAK ▲
Rosary Lakes
HIGHWAY 58
Davis Lake
Willamette Pass
Odell Lake

KILOMETRES 10 20 30

MILES 5 10 15

Warm Springs River
SKYLINE ROAD

PINHEAD BUTTES ▲
Lemiti Creek
Trooper Springs

Jude Lake
Russ Lake
OLALLIE BUTTE ▲
OLALLIE LAKE GUARD STATION
Breitenbush River
Olallie Lake (RESORT)

South Fork Breitenbush R.
PYRAMID BUTTE ▲

Jefferson Park
Russell Lake
Russell Creek

North Santiam River
Milk Creek
MOUNT JEFFERSON
Pamelia Lake
Shales Lake

Marion Lake
Rockpile Lake

MOUNT JEFFERSON WILDERNESS
WARM SPRINGS INDIAN RESERVATION

Minto Pass

THREE FINGERED JACK ▲

LODGE
Santiam Pass
HIGHWAY 20

Big Lake
Coldwater Spring
MOUNT WASHINGTON WILDERNESS
MOUNT WASHINGTON ▲
BELKNAP CRATER ▲
HIGHWAY 242

KILOMETRES 10 20 30

54

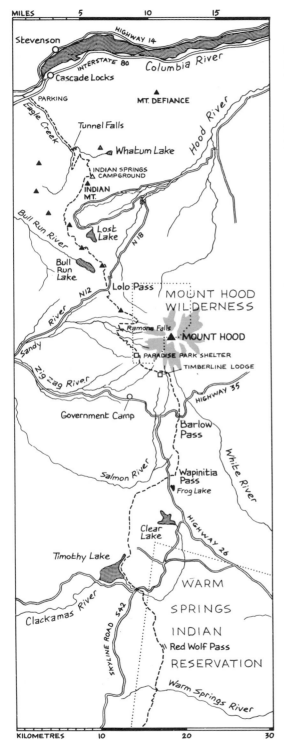

nature of the terrain, this is also an easy walk even though it is one of the longest in the book. One reason for this is that, as several roads cross the Cascades and a number of small resorts lie on or near to the trail, resupplying is not a problem. Another, and perhaps for some more important reason, is that there is very little climbing to be done. The route wanders along between 4,500 and 6,000ft (1,350 and 1,800m) for most of its length with just a few gentle climbs. Only on the section that traverses the slopes of Mount Hood near the end of the walk are there any steep climbs. Most of the time the route stays on or below timberline, passing by, rather than on, the volcanoes although on a few occasions slopes of lava and cinders are crossed as on Collier Cone and Belknap Crater. There is a good trail for the whole length of the trek, with all junctions clearly signposted. This means that it is a walk for the backpacker who wants to travel deep into the wilderness, but who doesn't want to deal with thousands of feet of ascent or difficult cross-country travel. It also means that a faster pace can be maintained than on some of the other walks and it should be possible to complete the distance in two weeks or less. The only problems you may encounter on the walk are mosquitos and water, as there are far too many of the former but surprisingly often not enough of the latter, with sources anything up to 22 miles (35.2km) apart.

The walk starts at a trailhead on Highway 58 just south-east of Williamette Pass. The initial 2 miles (3.2km) of easy forest walking leads to South, Middle and North Rosary Lakes, the first of the many lakes and pools to be encountered on this trek. The most impressive of the Rosary Lakes is Middle, which has the 400ft (120m) sheer cliff of Rosary Rock towering above it. There are many campsites in the woods near the lakes, although when I was there in mid-August, a vast number of boy scouts were scattered all over the area.

However, there are numerous other sites beside small creeks and little lakes in the next few miles (many of them named; I particularly liked Wait Here Camp even though I didn't!), so finding a quiet one is not too hard. Note though, that after Bobby Lake, just over 9 miles (14.4km) into the walk, there is no more water for nearly 8 miles (12.8km), so this is a good place for the first camp of the walk unless you want a long first day out. Bobby Lake lies ¼ mile (0.4km) to the east of the main route along the Moore Creek Trail. The large number of lakes does mean large numbers of mosquitos and even in mid-August, well after the peak of the mosquito season, there were plenty of them about. A tent with an insect-netting door is a good idea, as is repellent and tightly woven clothing that they can't bite through.

Alternating dense mountain hemlock and sparse lodgepole pine forest lines the trail for the next couple of days walking. Watch out for the otters that frequent the many ponds the trail passes. Twice I was able to sit quietly on the bank while otters swam and dived in the shallow waters close to me, a magical wilderness experience I felt privileged to be granted. Twenty-four and a half miles (39.2km) from the highway the Three Sisters Wilderness is entered. Permits are required but there is a self-issuing box on the trail, so obtaining one is no problem. The same applies to all the wilderness areas passed through on this walk. Remember, too, that in wilderness areas camping within 100ft (30m) of any lake is not allowed. Despite this, possible campsites still abound and my second one was on the dry open space of Cougar Flat with water drawn from a nearby pond. Twenty miles into the Three Sisters Wilderness there is a junction with the Island Meadows Trail a mile down which is Cascade Lakes Highway 46, paralleling the southern part of the trek, and Elk Lake Lodge, where meals and a limited selection of supplies can be bought.

*North Sister, Three Sisters Wilderness.*

A mile and a half (2.4km) beyond the junction our route starts to climb the western slope of Koosah Mountain from whose ridge you get your first inspiring view of the volcanoes as conical Bachelor Butte (9,065ft/ 2719.5m), jagged Broken Top (9,175ft/ 2,752.5m) and red rock capped South Sister (10,358ft/3,107.4m) appear soaring above the forest to the north-east, and beyond them Middle Sister (10,047ft/3,014.1m) and North Sister (10,085ft/3,025.5m). This vista gives a spur to the walking after all those miles in the pleasant but little-changing forest. It's only a taste of what is to come, however, as the trail immediately plunges back down into the trees and on to Camelot and Sisters Mirror Lakes. I

camped in a small grove of trees near the latter lake and spent the evening, along with several other campers, admiring the view of South Sister. Gray jays, ever present at popular sites, fluttered round looking for titbits. As dusk fell I was startled by an approaching walker who greeted me by name. I peered into the darkness. Walking towards me was PCT hiker Wayne Fuiten of Seattle who I'd last seen three months before when we'd met in the northern Mohave Desert. Since then, he'd taken a few weeks off from the trail, while the bulk of the winter's snow melted, and then continued his walk. My astonishment wasn't matched by his, as Wayne had been seeing my name in trail registers for the last few weeks and was expecting to catch up with me. One of the joys of long distance walking is swapping experiences

with other hikers you meet and Wayne and I sat long into the night recounting all that had happened since we last shared a campsite.

The route now enters the heart of the Three Sisters Wilderness and the next 20 plus miles are spectacular as the trail passes through meadows, forests and sparse parkland like tree-scattered uplands under the soaring summits of the Three Sisters themselves. Glaciers and snowfields decorate the sides of the mountains, while curling tongues of solidified lava floes and great heaps of black and red cinders tumble down into the forests and meadows, clear signs of the volcanic origins of this landscape. Once past the Sisters the switchbacking trail, crunchy underfoot now, leads up one of the frozen basalt flows towards a clear breach in the walls of Collier Cone before turning off north over more lava ridges and through scanty timberline trees to 6,040ft (1,812m) Scott Pass and South Matthieu Lake, where there are scenic if exposed campsites. As there is no more water on the trail for nearly 14 miles (22.4km) this is a good place to stop.

From the lake, the route continues over the lavafields to the McKenzie Highway and entry to the Mount Washington Wilderness. A climb up the rough black and red cinders of Belknap Crater takes us to a col from where the shining spires of Mount Washington (7,794ft/2,338.2m), Three-Fingered Jack (7,841ft/2,352.3m), Mount Jefferson (10,497ft/3,149.1m) and, faintly in the far distance, Mount Hood (11,235ft/3,370.5m) can be seen spread out in a long line to the north; another inspirational view. The landscape immediately around you is one of barren desolation, all crumbling rock and disintegrating lava. Then trees reappear as the trail rounds the western slopes of Mount Washington to reach the welcome, refreshing waters of piped Cold-water Spring (which can apparently dry up in late summer when the campsites here are popular with mountaineers intent on climbing Mount Washington). Again, there is no more water on the trail for a long way, 21½ miles (34.4km) in fact.

However, 7½ miles (12km) from the spring is 4,810ft (1,443m) Santiam Pass and the Santiam Highway. Half a mile (0.8km) down this road to the west lies Santiam Lodge, a church camp and Youth Hostel offering meals, showers and lodging; a good place to stay. Supplies can be sent here too, the address being Santiam Lodge, Star Route, Sisters, OR 97759. There is a small holding charge. Between Cold-water Spring and Santiam Pass, the route descends into the forest and then passes through a large area of burned lodgepole pine infested, when I was there, with mosquitos. It's worth pushing on to the lodge once you've passed the spring. The lack of water in the area between was confirmed by a hiker named Mark

I met as I was leaving the lodge. Dark having caught him out, he'd camped 4 miles back and had found no water at all despite a diligent search. As he hadn't been carrying any, he'd had a thirsty and hungry night (all his food was dehydrated) and he arrived at the lodge desperate for a drink and something to eat. As it's still 14 miles (22.4km) to the next water apart from a few shallow and unappetizing looking pools, full bottles should be carried from the lodge.

The Mount Jefferson Wilderness is entered once the Santiam Highway is crossed, but the mountain the trail first climbs towards is Three-Fingered Jack, whose distinctive serrated crest has far more than three spires when seen from the south. After traversing the slopes west of the peak, you can look back to the north side and see how the peak came by its name, as well as admire the convoluted red strata of this volcanic remnant. Once past the peak, the trail descends again and follows a wooded ridge to Rockpile Lake. Camping by the lake is forbidden, but there are plenty of sites in the nearby woods. Myriad mosquitoes and a heavy thunderstorm had me sheltering in the tent all evening here, despite the scenic surroundings.

Three miles (4.8km) after leaving Rockpile Lake, Mount Jefferson comes into view. This soaring, shapely, pointed peak, in my view the most impressive of the Oregon Cascades, is to stay in sight for most of the next 20 miles (32km) as a wonderful timberline walk begins. There are many campsites by the lakes and in the meadows along the west side of the peak, but this is a very popular area and many have been overused and subsequently closed. Great care should be taken to minimize the impact of camping in the fragile terrain in this wilderness area. Shale Lake, 6 miles (9.6km) on from Rockpile Lake, is a case in point. It's clear why so many people have camped here, but also clear why this is now forbidden. A long gentle descent leads from Shale Lake to Milk Creek, an aptly-named glacial outflow stream, and a walk across a series of avalanche gullies and glacier melt-fed creeks, many of which have to be forded. Most of the crossings are easy, but Russell Creek should be forded during the morning as on hot afternoons it can turn into a savage torrent. People have been drowned here as there is a deep gorge below the ford, but when I crossed it, the water was only ankle deep.

After the ford, the flat, wide and beautiful expanse of Jefferson Park with its tree groves, flower meadows and lakes backed by the glaciers and barren slopes of Mount Jefferson is reached. This is, understandably, the most popular spot in this wilderness area, so if you camp here it's important to keep away from the lakes and delicate meadows. I camped on a hard-packed, well-used site not far from Russell Lake in a grove of trees. A wonderful, calm evening ensued, with subtle shades of pink and blue across the sky as the rays of the setting sun spread across the lake and lit up the snowfields of Mount Jefferson. The only irritations in this idyllic spot were, again, the mosquitoes and also the after-dark cries of late-arriving campers. 'Anyone here with the Mazamas?' The unanswered question rang round the meadows over and over again, now loud, now faint, eventually abandoned as the callers settled down for the night. The Mazamas, I learnt later, is the name of an Oregon mountaineering club.

A thousand foot climb on which snow patches may still be present in late August leads up to Park Ridge at 6,920ft (2,076m) from which there are superb views of Jefferson Park and Mount Jefferson. The sadness I felt at leaving this sublime area was mitigated by the view to the north of towering Mount Hood. To the west of it I could see the recently active Mount St Helens in southern Washington, a plume of smoke still trailing from its ruptured summit cone in 1982. After a long, last look across the Mount Jefferson Wilderness, the

*A curious trail sign – the nearest water really is four miles in either direction!*

lengthy descent back into the forest over glacial rubble and large snow patches is undertaken. Leaving the wilderness area behind the trail reaches and then parallels Skyline Road S42 to the Olallie Lake Guard Station, a few yards from Head Lake. A short distance along the road from here is Olallie Lake Resort, where limited supplies can be purchased. I lunched here on Coca-Cola and doughnuts and supplemented my supplies with trail mix and candy bars. The next supply point is at Timberline Lodge on the slopes of Mount Hood, another 54 miles further on, so it's worth stocking up with a few extra goodies here. There is an excellent view along Olallie Lake to the distant cone of Mount Jefferson.

The trail is now firmly back in the forest again, as it enters the Warm Springs Indian Reservation and passes Russ and Jude Lakes, by which there are campsites. Jude Lake marks the last water until the trail descends to Lemiti Creek, nearly 6 miles (9.6km) away. There are campsites by the creek, but better ones and purer water are to be found down a half mile

Mount Washington, Three-Fingered Jack, Mount Jefferson and, faintly, Mount Hood
line up above the forest.

The author and Mount Jefferson.

*Mount Hood.*

(0.8km) spur trail near the large hole of Trooper Springs where I camped with Wayne who I'd met again during the late afternoon. Again there is no water for a further 8 miles (12.8km). The shady forest walking prevents overheating however, as the route traverses the slopes of several wooded hills with just the occasional glimpse of Mounts Hood and Jefferson to the north and south respectively. Halfway between the water sources on the trail over one of these hills, North Pinhead Butte, there is a sign, obviously placed by a trail crew with a sense of humour, bearing the question 'Thirsty?' Underneath it says 'Water 4' with arrows pointing in both directions. Actually, the next water is four miles to the north and is a tiny spring of doubtful quality that lies a few yards down a spur trail. In just over another 2 miles (3.2km) however, the bridged Warm Springs River is reached, providing ample water and a good campsite. Here, at latitude 45° north, you are halfway between the Equator

and the North Pole. Uneventful forest walking continues past various minor roads which lead west to the Skyline Road and campgrounds along Clackamas and Timothy Lakes. I camped by the latter lake, but near the trail and away from the vehicle camps.

Fifteen more miles (24km) of forest have to be traversed to Highway 35 and entry to the Mount Hood region. This forest, especially in the section above the Salmon River, is impressive and diverse with lodgepole and western white pine, Douglas fir, western hemlock, western red cedar, alaska cedar and silver, grand and noble firs. A spring just beyond the Linney Creek Road, 4 miles (6.4km) after leaving Timothy Lake, is the last guaranteed water on the trail until the upper Salmon River is reached, after another 14 miles (22.4km). However after 5 more miles (8km) the Frog Lake Road can be followed for ½ mile to Frog Lake Campground and a water source. Heading east now the trail crosses Highway 26 and then reaches the 4,157ft (1,247m) Barlow Pass. The old road running through the pass follows the line of the first road ever built over the Cascades in 1845–1846. Just beyond the pass the current road, Highway 35, is reached. Six miles (9.6m) down the old road from Barlow Pass lies Government Camp, where there is a store and a post office (zip code OR 97028). It is better to mail supplies to the Ski Shop at Timberline Lodge (also OR 97028) which lies on the trail 5 miles (8km) ahead, but there is a holding charge.

To reach the lodge from Highway 35, the trail climbs for 1,800ft (540m), the longest continuous ascent of the walk, crossing the upper Salmon River and the first on-trail water since the Linney Creek Road spring. The last 2 miles (3.2km) of the climb are on a sandy ridge above timberline with excellent views of Mount Hood, Oregon's highest peak. Timberline Lodge is an imposing stone and timber structure built in the 1930s and now mainly used by skiers. The downhill skiing facilities on the glaciers of Mount Hood are open year-round. I had a food parcel to collect at the lodge and I also ate a good, if expensive, meal there. Real food was so welcome that I bivvied out under the trees not far away and went back the next morning for breakfast!

For the first 16 miles (25.6km) beyond the lodge, our route follows the 40-mile (64-km) Timberline Trail which encircles Mount Hood. With many ups and downs in and out of the multiplicity of glacial stream channels, this is the most strenuous part of the walk, but also one of the grandest. As I set off on the trail from the lodge, I could see skiers on the one area of runs still open in late August, that closed by 1.30pm at this time of year due to the danger of avalanche. After 3 miles (4.8km) the Mount Hood Wilderness is reached and an alpine world is entered, as views open up of Mount Hood's icefalls, cliffs, glaciers, hanging valleys and meltwater creeks, several of which tumble down the loose slopes in gushing cascades.

A bizarre, though perhaps typically American, encounter occurred as I reached the top of a ridge in this section. A backpacker was sitting there looking at the view. As I approached he turned to reveal, quite deliberately, a large holstered pistol on his hip. Instead of commenting on the scenery or the trail, he immediately launched into an explanation of why he was 'packing iron', as he called it. 'You never know when you might have to shoot someone,' he said as though this happened several times a day, before expressing clear shock that I wasn't carrying a gun! As with other weapon-carrying people I've met in the American mountains, he was very friendly and not at all threatening. He just seemed obsessed with the idea that there were hordes of people out in the wilderness waiting to shoot him. I continued the walk slightly baffled by this seemingly paranoid attitude.

When you can wrench your eyes away from Mount Hood, there are views from the higher points on the trail all the way back to Mount Jefferson and the Three Sisters and, in Washington to the north, the white bulk of Mount Adams (see Chapter 5). There are several potential campsites along the trail plus, 4½ miles (7.2km) from the lodge, the Paradise Park Shelter, constructed from lava blocks. Beyond the shelter, the trail switchbacks down towards the forest but the superb scenery continues as the cliff-girt canyon down which pours Sandy River Falls and the rock walls of Slide Mountain and Rushing Water Creek canyon come into view. A good campsite called Scout Camp lies at the bottom of the switchbacks beside Rushing Water Creek, after the trail has left the Mount Hood Wilderness. The trail then crosses the Sandy River, passes by pretty Ramona Falls and climbs upwards again back into the Wilderness. After a few more miles leave the Timberline Trail and the slopes of Mount Hood and start a descent that is to last for the rest of the walk. At 3,420ft (1,026m) Lola Pass, a flat area with views of Mount Hood, makes for a good campsite, though it is close to a dirt road. Water can be found running near the road a ¼ mile (0.4km) to the west.

From the pass, an undulating wooded ridge walk leads to a traverse of the open stony slopes of Indian Mountain from which can be seen Mount Adams, Mount St Helens and distant Mount Rainier which, at 14,410ft (4,323m) is the highest peak in the Cascades. A descent leads to Indian Springs Campground, reachable by a very rough road. There are two routes from here to the Eagle Creek valley. The quickest is to descend the unmaintained Indian Springs Trail for 2 miles (3.2km) and 1,500ft (450m) to the Eagle Creek Trail, but this I found out, is a very steep, overgrown and knee-jarring trail. Easier but longer, is to stay on the Pacific Crest Trail for another 2½ miles (4km) as it gently descends to a junction with the Eagle Creek Trail near Wahtum Lake. Another 2½ miles (4km) down the latter trail and the junction with the Indian Springs Trail is met.

The short Eagle Creek Trail is totally enclosed by forest and yet is a dramatic and unusual walk. At first there is no sign of the grandeur to come, as the trail descends for 3½ miles (5.6km) to 7½ Mile Camp which boasts a crude shelter and would be a good place to stop. I went on, however, as I wanted to reach Eagle Creek in the late afternoon for photographic reasons. Three-quarters of a mile (1.2km) further on, the creek is reached and the highlights of the route begin, as a series of ever more spectacular waterfalls appears. The trail itself is impressive and exhilarating, for long sections narrow and exposed, running high above the creek on a shelf blasted out of the sheer cliffs.

After passing by a 100ft (30m) two-drop waterfall tumbling down a narrow ravine, the trail rounds a corner and there ahead is the fantastic sight of the 150ft (45m) sheer drop of Tunnel Falls with the trail apparently running straight into the falling water. However, as the name suggests, there *is* a tunnel in the rock behind the torrent through which you can walk. The East Fork of Eagle Creek has here carved a massive amphitheatre in the cliffs as it crashes down to join the main stream below. As you approach the falls, the noise is thunderous and the spray drenching and cold. Sections of chain run along the damp cliff walls, green with moss and ferns, for you to hold on to. Passing through the dark, damp tunnel, knowing that only a few feet of rock separates you from the power of the falls, is a strange and exciting experience. The reason for being here during the afternoon is that the falls face west and only then do they catch the sun's rays. I'd arranged to meet Wayne, who I'd now encountered several times during the walk since meeting him at Sisters Mirror Lake, here so that we could photograph each other by the falls, our figures helping to show the scale. The sun was in just the right position so an orgy of picture-taking ensued. The area is so beautiful and dramatic that I had no desire to move on and spent some time wandering back and forth through the tunnel.

Waterfalls abound as the trail continues down beside Eagle Creek and past Blue Ridge Camp, a pleasant spot where Wayne and I camped. Due to the popularity of the trail, camping is only allowed on designated sites, of which there are several. Although there is no official wilderness designation for the area, the Forest Service maintains the 50,000 acres around Eagle Creek as a roadless area. From Blue Ridge Camp, it's only 6 miles (9.6km) to the trailhead and the end of the trek, but these last few miles are so scenic that it's worth taking some time over them. A final steep and narrow section of trail climbs high above the creek, with more chains to hold on to for

*The author by a Pacific Crest Trail marker on Belknap Crater, Mount Washington in the background.*

safety, before the trailhead and highway are reached in the Columbia River valley. If no transport has been arranged, another 2½ miles (4km) of trail will take you to Interstate 80N and the town of Cascade Locks. From here, buses can be taken out of the mountains, but for those who haven't yet had enough of the volcanic scenery of the Cascades and shudder at the thought of returning to civilization, a link can easily be made to the walk described in Chapter 5 and you can have the enjoyment of another few weeks spent in the sane world of the mountains.

*Sandy River Falls, Mount Hood Wilderness.*

## THE ROUTE

| MILEAGE/(KM) | | PLACE | ELEVATION ft | m |
|---|---|---|---|---|
| 0.0 | 0.0 | Highway 58 near Williamette Pass | 5,090 | 1,527 |
| 2.6 | 4.1 | Middle Rosary Lake | 5,830 | 1,749 |
| 9.2 | 14.7 | Bobby Lake | 5,470 | 1,641 |
| 24.5 | 39.2 | Three Sisters Wilderness boundary | 5,730 | 1,719 |
| 31.6 | 50.5 | Cougar Flat | 5,750 | 1,725 |
| 38.2 | 61.1 | Island Lake | 5,438 | 1,631.4 |
| 44.7 | 71.5 | Island Meadow Trail | 5,250 | 1,575 |
| 50.6 | 80.9 | Sisters Mirror Lake | 5,995 | 1,798.5 |
| 71.6 | 114.5 | South Matthieu Lake | 6,040 | 1,812 |
| 75.7 | 121.1 | Highway 242 at McKenzie Pass | 5,280 | 1,584 |
| 93.0 | 148.8 | Highway 20 at Santiam Pass | 4,810 | 1,443 |
| 106.9 | 171.0 | Rockpile Lake | 6,250 | 1,875 |
| 115.2 | 184.3 | Shale Lake | 5,910 | 1,773 |
| 127.1 | 203.3 | Russell Lake | 5,856 | 1,756.8 |
| 139.5 | 223.2 | Olallie Lake Guard Station | 4,950 | 1,485 |
| 149.7 | 239.5 | Trooper Springs | 4,400 | 1,320 |
| 160.3 | 256.4 | Warm Springs River | 3,330 | 999 |
| 172.7 | 276.3 | Timothy Lake | 3,220 | 966 |
| 188.5 | 301.6 | Highway 35 near Barlow Pass | 4,155 | 1,246.5 |
| 193.2 | 309.1 | Timberline Lodge | 5,940 | 1,782 |
| 204.1 | 326.5 | Ramona Falls | 3,460 | 1,038 |
| 212.2 | 339.5 | Lola Pass | 3,420 | 1,026 |
| 224.7 | 359.5 | Indian Springs Campground | 4,300 | 1,290 |
| 226.7 | 362.7 | Eagle Creek Trail | 2,800 | 840 |
| 231.4 | 370.2 | Tunnel Falls | 1,120 | 336 |
| 237.6 | 380.1 | Eagle Creek Trail parking lot | 150 | 45 |

The trailhead is ¼ mile south-east of **Williamette Pass** on **Highway 58** (5,090ft, Mile 0). From here the trail, signed Pacific Crest Trail, climbs steadily to the three **Rosary Lakes** (5,830ft, Mile 2.6), crosses a saddle (6,170ft), then descends to junctions with the **Bobby Lake** and Moore Creek Trails (5,470ft, Mile 9.2). Bobby Lake lies ¼ mile east down the latter trail. The undulating forest trail continues past several shaded pools entering the **Three Peaks Wilderness** (5,730ft, Mile 24.5), passing open **Cougar Flat** (5,750ft, Mile 31.6), to a junction with the **Island Meadows Trail** (5,250ft, Mile 44.7), a mile down which lies Elk Lake Lodge. The lake-dotted trail meanders on to finally provide a view of the mountains from the slopes of Koosah Mountain before reaching Camelot and **Sisters Mirror Lakes** (5,995ft, Mile 50.6). A mile further and the route begins a timberline traverse below the Three Sisters themselves on Wickiup Plain. There are many trail junctions in this section but all are well marked. Leaving the meadows, the route then climbs over rough lava floes and cinder cones to Scott Pass and **South Matthieu Lake** (6,040ft, Mile 71.6). Four more miles of walking on or close to the lava beds leads to **McKenzie Pass** (5,280ft, Mile 75.7) and Highway 242 where the route departs from the Three Sisters Wilderness and enters the Mount Washington Wilderness. The trail now goes up the large lava flows of Belknap Crater to a saddle (6,120ft) and then back into forest to round

Mount Washington on its west side and arrive at Coldwater Spring (5,200ft, Mile 85.4). A continuing descent leads to **Highway 20 at Santiam Pass** (4,810ft, Mile 93). Down the road to the west lies Santiam Lodge. A mile and a half after the pass the trail, climbing now, enters the Mount Jefferson Wilderness and traverses the lower slopes of Three-Fingered Jack before descending to Minto Pass and then climbing to **Rockpile Lake** (6250ft, Mile 106.9). Continuing north in and out of the forest, the trail heads for Mount Jefferson, crossing the lower slopes of the Cathedral Rocks to **Shale Lake** (5,910ft, Mile 115.2) and then descending to Milk Creek (4320ft). Passing to the west of Mount Jefferson, the trail comes to a potentially difficult ford of glacier-fed Russell Creek beyond which we enter Jefferson Park and reach **Russell Lake** (5,856ft, Mile 127.1). After fording the South Fork Breitenbush River, the trail climbs up to Park Ridge (6,920ft), then descends to the Skyline Road and **Olallie Lake Guard Station** (4,950ft, Mile 139.5). Olallie Lake Resort lies a short distance down this road. Back in forest again the trail is now in the Warm Springs Indian Reservation as it passes Jude Lake and crosses Lemiti Creek, a few hundred yards beyond which lies **Trooper Springs** (4,400ft, Mile 149.7). After crossing the **Warm Springs River** (3,330ft, Mile 160.3), at 45° north the trail passes large **Timothy Lake** (3,220ft, Mile 172.7) to finally start climbing out of the trees again at **Highway 35 near Barlow Pass** (4,155ft, Mile 188.5). After crossing the upper Salmon River, **Timberline Lodge** on the slopes of Mount Hood is reached (5,940ft, Mile 193.2). A switchbacking route round the west side of the mountain now begins, entering the Mount Hood Wilderness at the Zigzag River. Paradise Park Shelter is passed, then the Sandy River crossed and **Ramona Falls** reached (3,460ft, Mile 204.1). After crossing Muddy Fork the trail heads away from Mount Hood crosses **Lola Pass** (3,420ft, Mile 212.2) and arrives at the **Indian Springs Campground** (4,300ft, Mile 224.7), where there is a choice of routes. The easier but longer route is to continue on the PCT for 2½ miles to a junction with the Eagle Creek Trail at Wahtum Lake. The more direct route is to descend the unmaintained Indian Springs Trail for 2 miles, to meet the **Eagle Creek Trail** 2½ miles down from the Wahtum Lake junction. The Eagle Creek Trail is then followed down past **Tunnel Falls** to the trailhead **parking lot** (150ft, Mile 237.6).

## GUIDEBOOK AND MAPS

*The Pacific Crest Trail Volume 2: Oregon and Washington* by Jeffrey P. Schaffer and A. Selters (Wilderness Press) contains 1:50,000 topographic maps for the whole route with the trail marked on them, plus larger scale maps for overviews of the area and the locations of roads and services. These are all the maps required, although they could be supplemented with the 1:62,500 strip maps of the *Pacific Crest Trail Pocket Guide*.

# The Southern Washington Cascades:
## Panther Creek to Chinook Pass    139 miles (222km)

*Wilderness areas are first of all a series of sanctuaries for the primitive arts of wilderness travel.*

Aldo Leopold   A *Sand County Almanac*

To the north of the deep trench of the Columbia River gorge, the Cascade Mountains rise up again to run the length of the state of Washington and on into southern Canada, but the character of the range changes from that in Oregon. In the southern half of the state, the rolling wooded hills continue, interspersed with three huge volcanic peaks, Mounts Adams (12,286ft/3,685.8m), St Helens (9,677ft/2,903.1m) and Rainier (14,410ft/4,323m)). These do not line up close together as do the volcanoes of the northern Oregon Cascades, but stand truly isolated, miles apart, rising abruptly out of the forest. There are also far fewer subsidiary volcanic peaks although north of Mount Adams, the jagged ridges of the Goat Rocks Wilderness mark the remains of a once-

*Mount Adams and the Adams Glacier.*

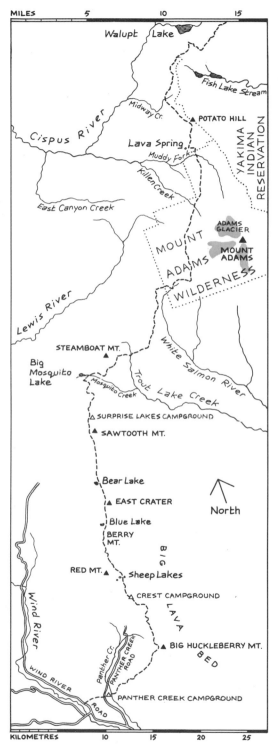

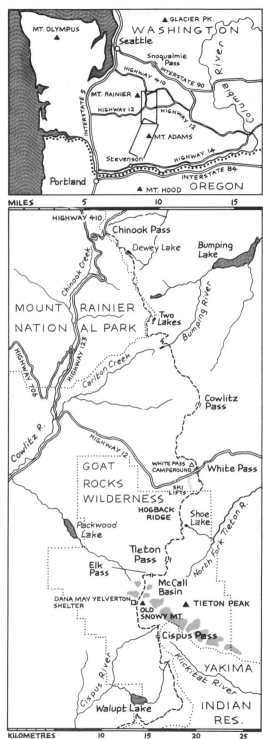

massive volcano. North of Rainier the wooded hills change into the complex and rugged mountains of the North Cascades (described in Chapter 7).

Although only 139 miles (222km) long, the walk through the southern Washington Cascades is a much tougher proposition than the trail through the Oregon Cascades, as there is far more ascent and descent, and in the Goat Rocks Wilderness there is a lengthy above timberline section along narrow ridges that could be difficult in bad weather and impassable when under snow. The climate is also wetter and more stormy as the area lies in the Pacific North West region, in the track of storms running down from the Arctic. To add to the difficulties, there are no supply points within reach of the route for the first 110 miles (176km). At White Pass there is a grocery store, lodging and post office (the address is White Pass, Naches, WA 98648). However, the paths are good as the Pacific Crest Trail is followed, so the walk should take no more than seven to ten days. My own trek took eight days. The scenery is magnificent with a total contrast between the first half of the walk when the trail, mostly below timberline, passes beneath the great bulk of Mount Adams, the middle part when it climbs high up on to the crest of the mountains in the Goat Rocks Wilderness and traverses across the Packwood Glacier and the last section where it follows a gentler ridge, the Cascade Crest, along the eastern perimeter of Mount Rainier National Park. Permits are only needed for the park if you're going to camp in it which isn't necessary.

The trailhead for the walk lies 10 miles (16km) from Highway 14 in the Columbia River valley up a side road at Panther Creek Campground. On the drive up here permits for the Mount Adams and Goat Rocks Wilderness Areas should be picked up from the Wind River Ranger Station, near the little settlement of Carson. If you want to get your permits in advance, write to Gifford Pinchot National Forest, 500 West 12th Street, Vancouver, WA 98660. In the wilderness areas, not only is it forbidden to camp within 100ft (30m) of any lake, but it's also forbidden to camp within 200ft (60m) of the Pacific Crest Trail. It's advisable to leave Panther Creek Campground with plenty of water, as it's 17 miles (27.2km) and 4000ft (1,200m) of ascent to the next guaranteed source, the murky and very dubious looking Sheep Lake. The first 3,000ft (900m) is gained in the first 8½ miles (13.6km) as the trail climbs Big Huckleberry Mountain.

Huge, flat-topped and glacier-strewn Mount Adams comes into view for the first time as the trail undulates through the forest north of Big Huckleberry. A legend of the Columbia River Indians about Mount Adams says that, along with his brother Mount Hood and the female Mount St Helens, he smoked continuously. Both brothers, sons of the Great Spirit, courted St Helens who eventually chose Adams. This so annoyed Hood that he struck his brother a huge blow on the head, leaving him with his current flat top and so cowed that he's never raised his head since! Certainly Adams is the only one of the Cascade volcanoes without a 'proper' summit cone, although the mountain makes up for that with its massive bulk and impressive glaciers.

Just over 10 miles (16km) from Panther Creek there is a gully which reputedly has a spring in it, but this was dry in late August so it shouldn't be relied upon. Crest Campground, 15 miles (24km) into the walk, looks a good site, but is dry. A dirt road gives vehicle access to this camp and it is much used by outfitters, as can be seen by the presence of several horse corrals. Unfortunately, although Sheep Lake is now only 2 miles (3.2km) away it's also 800ft (240m) higher. That was far enough for me so, despite the so-called lake being no more than a shallow muddy puddle, I camped here and drank the water, although not until I'd added purification tablets. If you really can't face using the filthy water here, another slightly larger and possibly cleaner pond called Green Lake lies a mile further along the trail. A storm swept in during the night I was at Sheep Lake and I spent the next two days and 33 miles (52.8km) walking in mist and rain, which rather coloured my views of this section of the trail. In sunny weather it's probably far less boring! There are, according to the guidebooks, good views at various points of Adams, Hood and St Helens but all were shrouded in cloud during my walk. Blue Lake, 5 miles (8km) beyond Sheep Lake, has clear water and there are good campsites nearby. I went on for another 14 miles (22.4km) past Junction Lake, Bear Lake and Deer Lake, by all of which there are campsites (the campsite at Surprise Lakes

is for Indians only), to camp by the clean outlet creek of Big Mosquito Lake.

The trail continues, still mainly in the forest, past various pools and creeks and possible campsites, before entering the Mount Adams Wilderness 49 miles (78.4km) into the walk. The rain had left the forest and the dense trailside vegetation sodden, so my walk along this section was very wet, even when it wasn't raining. As various forest roads reach to the edge of the Wilderness Area near here, the walk could be started at this point. Less than a mile after entering the Wilderness a broad, shallow and dry creek bed is encountered, graced confusingly with the grandiose name of White Salmon River. However, 50 yards (45m) below the trail, a powerful spring gushes out of the thick vegetation providing cold,

*The entrance to Mount Rainier National Park at Chinook Pass, at the end of the walk.*

refreshing water. As the next water lay 6½ miles (10.4km) away, I camped nearby. Luckily the clouds cleared overnight to give a heavy dew and a clear dawn sky. The fine weather was welcome, as the next 20 miles (32km) give good views of Mount Adams with the trail contouring at timberline below its massive western aspect.

The terrain immediately to hand is also attractive with many flower-filled meadows and groves of subalpine fir and mountain hemlock. Further ahead, frequent glimpses of the Goat Rocks and the squat white cone of Mount Rainier, wreathed with shreds of dirty cumulus clouds, could be seen, but dominating the view are the huge glaciers tumbling down the flanks of Mount Adams. As the walk progresses so views are obtained of White Salmon Glacier, Pinnacle Glacier and most impressive of all the steep, frozen, chaotic and broken giant ice-fall of Adams Glacier. The trail is softer and gentler than round Mount Hood as it stays just below the rugged slopes of the mountain itself, providing a view at a distance rather than the intimate contact with the guts of the peak that one experiences on Hood. I wandered along feeling calm and peaceful watching the mountain as if I were watching the sea from the safety of the shore. There was no sense of the immediacy, the urgency, or the fear often felt when high up in the mountains. Mount Adams was like a picture, part of a separate reality to the pleasant arcadia of the timberline scenery which I was actually walking through.

Sheep Lake, a reasonably sized and clean looking pool, is reached after 6½ miles (10.4km). Then comes a succession of milky glacier meltwater-fed creeks that have to be hopped across. Camps could be set up near most of them. I particularly liked the look of the site just after the crossing of Killen Creek

that lies in a tree grove beside a meadow and pretty waterfall. However, I pushed on with a gentle descent into the forest and out of the Mount Adams Wilderness. There are more campsites by bridged Muddy Fork, but less than ½ mile (0.8km) further on a beautifully clear and pure spring gushes out of the foot of a large crumbling lava flow. There is a campsite nearby, but even if you don't camp here, it's worth filling up your water bottles as Lava Spring provides some of the best water on any of the walks in this book. As I approached the spring, a deep rich red-brown pine marten darted across the trail a few feet in front of me with something in its mouth. These sudden glimpses of wild animals are one of the sublime joys of wilderness walking. A mile and a half beyond the spring, there is a section of dirt road walking that lasts until Midway Creek is reached, a couple of miles further on. Here, I camped on sandy soil under small, sparsely branched lodgepole pines.

The trail then passes a series of stagnant ponds whose water would need purifying before it could be drunk. Five miles (8km) from Midway Creek, the trail enters the Goat Rocks Wilderness after an 800ft (240m) climb through a mixture of forested and logged land. In less than a mile after entering the Wilderness, a 5,600ft (1,680m) ridgecrest is reached and a view of the glacier-clad slopes and rocky ridges of 7,930ft (2,379m) Old Snowy Mountain appears. The whole atmosphere of the walk changes in just a few miles. Suddenly your carefree stroll through the forest has turned into a challenging, high mountain trek. As I gazed at the steep, rugged landscape ahead, across which I knew the trail led, I felt the familiar buzz of excitement that comes before the start of a mountain climb. My pulse quickened as did my step, my relaxed mood abruptly shattered as I became impatient to stride along those narrow ridges.

A beautiful mixed forest of mountain hem-

*(Preceding pages) Shoe Lake from Hogback Ridge.*

lock and lodgepole pine, interspersed with several distinctive, wilted-looking Alaska cedars is encountered next, before the trail curves across open slopes above the Walupt Lake Basin, enters the forest again and arrives at Walupt Creek. There is nowhere flat enough for a camp here, but ½ mile (0.8km) further on, good sites can be found round yet another Sheep Lake.

The views open out now as the trail climbs above timberline to 6,460ft (1,938m) Cispus Pass, weaving either side of a ridge high above the deep, glaciated canyon of the Klickitat River, across which can be seen the barren rock and talus walls of Gilbert Peak. The nature of the landscape in the Goat Rocks Wilderness becomes clear during this ascent. Barren scree slopes and glacial run-off washes interspersed with flower-rich alpine meadows make up the lower slopes of the deep, glaciated cirques, while above rise shining white permanent snowfields topped by tiny rock peaks and narrow arêtes. From Cispus Pass, a short descent leads to the headwaters of the Cispus River where there is a campsite. A mile and a half further on, the trail starts the 2 mile (3.2km) 1,100ft (330m) climb to the west ridge of Old Snowy Mountain where, at an elevation of 7,040ft (2,112m) is found the tiny stone Dana May Yelverton Shelter. Halfway up this climb, a massive 40ft (12m) high boulder called Split Rock lies next to the trail; a boulder that is indeed split in two with full-size trees growing in the gap.

Dana May Yelverton Shelter is named after a hiker who died up here. When she became hypothermic, her friends put her in a sleeping bag and went for help, but when they returned they found her dead. They built the shelter as a memorial and created a marvellous place to stay. As I found, it gives adequate protection from the wind although the holes in the roof suggest it would leak in rain (the rule about not camping by the trail doesn't apply to the shelter). Around the 12ft² (3.6m²) earth-floored stone hut are stunted 4 to 10ft (1.2 to 3m) high hemlocks and whitebark pines. The view is magnificent. Across mile after mile of dark forest, sadly spotted now with the pale blocks of clear-cut areas, can be seen the white volcanic cones of Mounts Hood, St Helens and Rainier plus, immediately to hand, the heart of the Goat Rocks Wilderness. The evening I spent there, I wandered a little way up the ridge to sit and watch a bright moon rise over frozen Goat Lake as the last of the sun's pink rays faded from the sky. After all the camps down in the enclosed spaces of the forest, I felt an amazing sense of freedom at being up here surrounded by the vast black space of the mountain sky. So exhilarated did I feel, that I was up again to watch the dawn change from pink to deep red and then orange, and the rocks from black to sunlit grey.

From the shelter, the trail climbs imperceptibly for ¼ mile (0.4km) and 40ft (12m) to the 7,080ft (2,124m) high point of the route on a ridge above the glaciated 3000ft (900m) deep Upper Lake Creek canyon; above this ridge rise the summit slopes of Old Snowy Mountain. Although close to the shelter, this is such a marvellous situation that it's worth stopping for a minute to take in the dramatic scenery. The trail leaves the ridge here to cut across the top of the Packwood Glacier on a trail blasted out by the Forest Service in 1978, then drops down to a saddle at 6,850ft (2,055m). There follows the most impressive section of trail on the whole route as it follows a very narrow rocky ridge and contours round a series of jagged pinnacles to give a walk with real alpine character. One can only admire the efforts of the trail crew who built this high level route back in the 1950s. The views from the arête across the glistening ice of McCall Glacier to Tieton Peak at 7,768ft (2,330.4m) are magnificent. To the north-west Mount Rainier, much larger now, dominates the view. From a

*The Goat Rocks Wilderness.*

saddle, there is an exposed descent down an even narrower section of trail that is usually snowbound until the end of July, necessitating the use of crampons and ice axes. By 2 September when I was there, all the snow had long gone leaving just a thin dusty flat ribbon of trail snaking across the steep talus. A sign marked Cascade Crest Trail in the middle of this section warns horse riders and pack trains that there are no passing places for 1,000ft (300m) in one direction and 1,800ft (340m) in the other. If you see horses on this stretch of trail wait until they have completed it before you venture on to it. The ridge having been regained, Elk Pass at 6,680ft (2,004m), just over a mile from Dana May Yelverton Shelter, is reached and the descent east out of the Goat Rocks Wilderness is begun.

Half a mile (0.8km) down the descent ridge lie some exposed campsites on the first place flat enough for camping since well before Dana May Yelverton Shelter. Continuing to drop down through 3ft (0.9m) high timberline pines, the trail provides good views back to McCall Glacier before entering the forest proper. Soon afterwards, the extensive and popular meadows of McCall Basin are reached. There are several good, if well-used, campsites here. Note, however, that the trail turns sharply to the north just before the basin is entered. I missed this junction and ended up bushwhacking on a compass bearing through dense forest before picking up the trail again at Lutz Lake, a rather dispiriting and gloomy pond, only a mile (1.6km) from McCall Basin. It took me an hour to travel that distance cross-country. As I'd already spent an hour wandering around the meadow becoming increasingly frustrated and angry at my inability to locate the trail before giving up, I had plenty of pent-up energy to expend on the difficult task of clambering over endless fallen trees and

*McCall Glacier, Goat Rocks Wilderness.*

thrashing through thick clumps of bushes. I was in such a foul mood when I reached Lutz Lake that it was probably a good thing that I was on my own as this was an ideal situation for having a stupid row with someone. I had to make do with loudly cursing any bush that dared to appear in front of me and more quietly berating myself for not finding the path.

The trail goes on down to 4,570ft (1,371m) Tieton Pass but soon after that begins the 2,000ft (600m) climb to Hogback Ridge, a climb on which I was able to expend the last of my anger and negative feelings. From an open ridge on this ascent, there is a fine view of beautiful, pale blue Shoe Lake which looks a good place for a camp. So it would be, but for the fact that too many people have already thought the same, many without any idea of no-trace camping techniques. To prevent further degradation of the area, the Forest Service has closed it to camping. From the pleasant open traverse of Hogback Ridge, there are more views of the ever-nearer Mount Rainier. A forested descent leads down from the ridge to Highway 12, ½ mile (0.8km) north-east of 4,405ft (1321.5m) White Pass. At the pass there is a campground, ski lodge, café and the most welcome Cracker Barrel Grocery, source of the first supplies on the walk, which began a long 110 miles (176km) to the south. The store also boasts a post office and a laundrette. If you're running out of time or energy, this is a good place to end your walk. If instead you cannot resist the temptation of the views of Mount Rainier and want to see more of that peak, you'll continue for another 30 miles (48km).

Bivvying out on the White Pass Campground (for reasons of tiredness rather than desire, as I simply couldn't be bothered to erect the tent), I was woken by raucous bird calls as a flock of gray jays, plus a few of the bright blue Stellar's jays and a pair of hairy woodpeckers invaded the site. I then enjoyed the luxury of

breakfast in the café, where I was joined by a walker I'd met briefly several times over the last week. Jay J. Johnson was no ordinary walker however, as he was nearing the end of a 9,000 mile (14,400km) journey. Nearly nine months before he'd walked south along the 2,000 mile (3,200km) Appalachian Trail in eastern America, then rowed through the Everglades, cycled through Texas and started walking back north up the Pacific Crest Trail from the Mexican border. His journey would finish when he reached Canada and he admitted that all he now wanted to do was finish his marathon journey. He said that the spectacular surroundings now left him cold and he was taking whichever was the shortest route. Listening to him talk, I silently hoped that I would never become so fed up with travel in the mountains. Heavy rain began to fall so, not having had any time off from my Pacific Crest Trail walk for thirty-one days, I decided to stay here for a day, most of which I spent in the café talking to Jay and the other walkers who were there.

The rain continued all night, only stopping just as I set off, but thick clouds remained over the peaks. My main memory of the first 10 miles (16km) from White Pass is of the incredibly muddy and slippery state of the trail which had been churned to a quagmire by horses. Once across the bridged Bumping River the trail starts to climb into rugged alpine terrain and arrives at the boundary of Mount Rainier National Park. For the rest of the route, the trail follows the Cascade Crest which marks the eastern edge of the park. I enjoyed this high level trail with views into deep cirques and across to misty peaks, despite the weather. The trail crosses many steep slopes in this section which can be snowbound and hazardous with high avalanche danger until mid-July. The only slipperiness in early September, however, was caused by rain.

A short descent leads to a junction with the Two Lakes Trail 19 miles (30.4km) from White

Pass. Two Lakes, ⅓ mile (0.53km) down this trail, is a good place to camp and, as it's not in the park, a permit isn't required. This is also true of American and Dewey Lakes which lie not far ahead. From Two Lakes, a climb leads into the national park and some superb views of the overwhelming white mass of Mount Rainier, just 12 miles (19.2km) away, but 9,000ft (2,700m) higher. As well as being the highest peak in the Cascades at 14,410ft (4,323m), Rainier boasts the largest glacier system in the contiguous forty-eight states. There are twenty-six named glaciers. The park around the peak was created in 1899. In the park, the trail winds around ridges, through meadows and past crags along a narrow open crest, mostly out of the forest. Every turn brings another attractive vista. To the south can be seen Mount Adams and the Goat Rocks, sur-

prisingly distant now. Every so often the trail leaves the park and passes areas where 'permit-less' camping is possible with Dewey Lake providing the most attractive, but most used sites. The reason for this popularity is that the lake lies just under 3 miles (4.8km) from Chinook Pass and Highway 410, a scenic route through the Cascades from where it should be possible to hitch a lift if you haven't arranged transport. A log bridge over the road marks the entrance to the national park.

The keen backpacker with time and energy to spare may want to continue the walk for another 70 miles (112km) to Snoqualmie Pass and the start of the North Cascades route (Chapter 7). Unfortunately, large sections of the country between Chinook and Snoqualmie Passes have suffered clear-cut logging, so this walk cannot be recommended.

## THE ROUTE

| MILEAGE/(KM) | | PLACE | ELEVATION | |
|---|---|---|---|---|
| | | | ft | m |
| 0.0 | 0.0 | Panther Creek Campground | 930 | 279 |
| 8.7 | 13.9 | Big Huckleberry Mountain summit trail | 4,070 | 1,221 |
| 15.5 | 24.8 | Crest Campground | 3,490 | 1,047 |
| 17.4 | 27.8 | Sheep Lake | 4,020 | 1,206 |
| 22.9 | 36.6 | Blue Lake | 4,630 | 1,389 |
| 36.1 | 57.7 | Big Mosquito Lake outlet creek | 3,892 | 1,167.6 |
| 50.4 | 80.6 | White Salmon River | 4,900 | 1,470 |
| 62.2 | 99.5 | Killen Creek | 5,920 | 1,776 |
| 67.2 | 107.5 | Lava Spring | 4,520 | 1,356 |
| 75.3 | 120.4 | Midway Creek | 4,690 | 1,407 |
| 82.5 | 132 | Walupt Lake Trail | 4,960 | 1,488 |
| 89.9 | 143.8 | Cispus Pass | 6,460 | 1,938 |
| 93.6 | 149.7 | Dana May Yelverton Shelter | 7,040 | 2,112 |
| 97.9 | 156.6 | McCall Basin | 5,190 | 1,557 |
| 107.0 | 171.2 | White Pass Chair Lift trail | 5,830 | 1,749 |
| 110.4 | 176.6 | Highway 12 near White Pass | 4,405 | 1,321.5 |
| 123.3 | 197.2 | Bumping River | 4,080 | 1,224 |
| 129.8 | 207.6 | Two Lakes | 5,600 | 1,680 |
| 139.1 | 222.5 | Chinook Pass | 5,432 | 1,629.6 |

*Mount Rainier.*

To reach the trailhead, take the Wind River Road from Highway 14, 3 miles east of the town of Stevenson in the Columbia River valley for 5 miles, then turn up the Panther Creek Road to **Panther Creek Campground** (930ft, Mile 0) where the walk starts. The route here following the Old Huckleberry Trail, leaves the road 250yds south of the campground. It ascends immediately, switchbacking up Big Huckleberry Mountain and crossing a number of dirt roads, before arriving at a junction with the **Big Huckleberry Mountain summit trail** (4,070ft, Mile 8.7). The trail then meanders on through the forest, past a spring (3,550ft, Mile 10.4), to the waterless **Crest Campground** (3490ft, Mile 15.5). From here, the route signed Pacific Crest Trail climbs easily to muddy **Sheep Lake** (4,020ft, Mile 17.4). A mile beyond the lake, the trail switchbacks up the slopes of Berry Mountain and then drops slightly to to **Blue Lake** (4,630ft, Mile 22.9). Our route continues to undulate through the forest, past a number of pools and the Surprise Lakes Campground (for Indians only), before arriving at the **Big Mosquito Lake outlet creek** (3,892ft, Mile 36.1). After another 13½ wooded miles the trail enters the **Mount Adams Wilderness** (4,820ft, Mile 49.7) and soon afterwards crosses the often dry shallow bed of the **White Salmon River** (a spring can be found just below the trail). The trail then starts to climb in earnest to begin a northward traverse along the west side of Mount Adams across many glacial creeks. After crossing **Killen Creek** (5,920ft, Mile 62.2), the trail leaves the mountain behind, descends and returns to dense forest passing a lava floe out of which **Lava Spring** (4,520ft, Mile 67.2) gushes. **Midway Creek**

(4,690ft, Mile 75.3) is crossed 5 miles before the Goat Rocks Wilderness is entered. Open country is reached and a steep climb started after the junction with the **Walupt Lake Trail** (4,960ft, Mile 82.5) which leads over **Cispus Pass** to the **Dana May Yelverton Shelter** (7,040ft, Mile 93.6). A quarter of a mile further on, the trail traverses above the Packwood Glacier before following a narrow, rock ridge, down to Elk Pass (6,680ft). The continuing descent leads into the forest and to **McCall Basin** (5,190ft, Mile 97.9) and then Tieton Pass (4,570ft) before climbing again to a saddle (6,620ft) on Hogback Ridge, above Shoe Lake. A further descent then leads down to ski lifts and **Highway 12**, ½ mile north-east of **White Pass** (4,405ft, Mile 110.4). From the highway, the trail winds through the woods again to the bridged **Bumping River** (4,080ft, Mile 123.3), 3 miles beyond which we reach the Cascade Crest that is followed along the eastern edge of Mount Rainier National Park to the end of the walk at Highway 410 and **Chinook Pass** (5,432ft, Mile 139.1).

## GUIDEBOOK AND MAPS

*The Pacific Crest Trail Volume 2: Oregon and Washington* by Jeffrey P. Schaffer and A. Selters (Wilderness Press) contains 1:50,000 topographic maps for the whole route with the trail marked on them, plus larger scale maps for overviews of the area and the locations of road and services. These are all the maps needed, although they could be supplemented with the 1:62,500 strip maps of the *Pacific Crest Trail Pocket Guide*.

# Bob Marshall Country – The Northern Montana Rockies: Marias Pass to Rogers Pass
## 161 miles (258km)

*Thankfulness surged through me. Thankfulness for the moment, for the day, for the freedom of The Walk, for life itself.*

Colin Fletcher   *The Thousand Mile Summer*

The largest roadless area in the Rocky Mountains of the USA lies near the northern end of the range in the state of Montana. Most of this huge 1.5 million acres of mountain and forest is taken up by the Bob Marshall, Scapegoat and Great Bear Wildernesses. There are no roads across the mountains between US Highway 2 in the north and Montana Highway 200 in the south, a straight line distance of more than 100 miles (160km). The Continental Divide winds

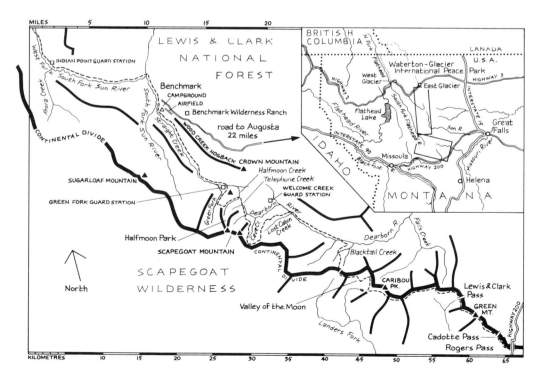

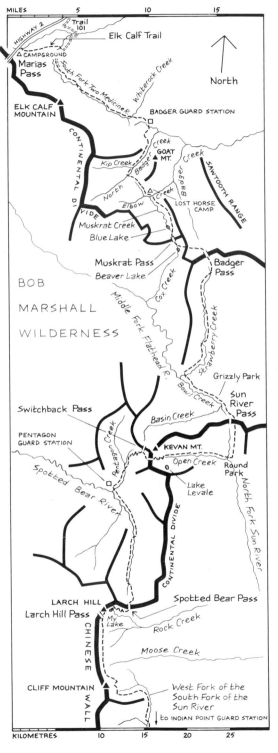

for over 200 miles (320km) down the centre of the region, twisting and turning along the top of the massive limestone cliffs that typify the landscape here. Either side of these cliffs, the biggest and most famous of which is the 1,000ft (300m) high, 13-mile (20.8-km) long Chinese Wall (so called apparently because it looks like the Great Wall of China, although no one knows who named it) in the centre of the Bob Marshall Wilderness, lie subalpine bowls, deep canyons, rushing rivers and mile after mile of pristine forest. These features give the area a distinct character very different from Glacier National Park on the other side of US 2, whose classic alpine scenery is really the southern extension of the Canadian Rockies, and the lower, wooded terrain found south of Rogers Pass on Highway 200. The vastness of this wilderness has allowed wildlife that has disappeared from most of the USA Rockies to survive here, species including grizzly bears, black bears, wolves, wolverines, and cougars, although there's not much chance of seeing any of these. In my view, it's enough just to know they're out there. The knowledge of their presence adds an indefinable quality to the wilderness, which is lacking in more tamed areas.

The largest wilderness area in this region is named for Bob Marshall, a pioneer conservationist employed by the Forest Service in the 1920s and 1930s who used his position to work to protect roadless areas, 14 million acres of which became designated wilderness during this time. A prodigious walker, often covering 30 miles (48km) a day, he wanted to see wildernesses where people could travel for two weeks at a time without crossing a road. A year after his death in 1939 such a wilderness was created in his honour, the 1,009,000-acre Bob Marshall Wilderness, known to *aficionados* as 'The Bob'. Adjacent to this wilderness to the south is the 240,000 acre Scapegoat Wilderness, created in 1972.

*Scott Steiner fording Strawberry Creek . . .*

*. . . and surveying the Chinese Wall (both Bob Marshall Wilderness).*

Any walk in these remote wildernesses is a serious affair. There are no easy or quick routes out of the heartland of the region. Our route traverses the Bob Marshall and Scapegoat Wildernesses from north to south, a distance of 161 miles (257.6km). There is only one possible supply point along this route. This lies 101 miles (161.6km) into the walk where the end of a dirt road is reached at Benchmark. Three miles down this road lies the Benchmark Wilderness Ranch which, for a fee, will hold parcels for hikers (the address is Bev and Bud Heckman, Benchmark Wilderness Ranch, Augusta, MT 59410). Although much of the walking is in fairly flat, forested river valleys, there are a number of steep ascents which can be difficult early in the season, when patches of snow still lie on the trails. An ice axe is then a useful accessory. As most of the rivers aren't bridged, fords can be deep and hazardous during snowmelt and a rope could be required. I walked the route in mid-June and, although some of the creeks were difficult to cross and a third leg (I used a ski pole) was essential, the rope my companion and I carried was never needed. The trails for most of the route are good (they are regularly used by horse parties), with junctions signposted, but for the last 40 miles (64km), much of the route is cross-country and care is needed with navigation, especially in bad weather. This is a walk for the experienced backpacker who likes remote and lonely country and you won't meet the crowds here that are to be found on the John Muir Trail or in the Oregon Cascades. Two weeks should be ample time for the trek and both ends of the route can be reached by public transport.

The best place to start the route is probably at Marias Pass itself on US Highway 2 near the Summit Campground, from where the Elk Calf Trail leads down to the South Fork of the Two Medicine River. Having walked from Glacier National Park, I started the route 4 miles (6.4km) east of the pass at a dirt road signed for Trail 101, the Two Medicine-Heart Butte Trail, which leads on dirt roads open for vehicle access past the Rising Wolf Ranch, via a fairly complicated route through several locked and barred gates, for 4 miles (6.4km) to where the Elk Calf Trail joins it. Apart from the care needed not to take a wrong turning up one of the many side tracks, there is a bridge across the South Fork of the Two Medicine River on the route I took that can only be described as heart-stopping. It consists of a single, large log, across which have been nailed a series of fairly widely-spaced short planks, which rock from side to side as you step on them. There is no hand rail, except for a worse than useless loose rope and far below, the river foams through a narrow rocky gorge. It took me four attempts to cross this bridge and I would not like to have to do it again. Some people we met later had taken one look at it and decided instead to make a difficult roped ford of the river below the gorge. The Elk Calf Trail avoids all this.

From the junction, Trail 101 is followed as it winds above the river through wooded terrain with some good views of Elk Calf Mountain. There are several potential campsites. My American companion, Scott Steiner, and I pitched our tent on a shingle bank next to the shimmering river after 8 miles (12.8km), a beautiful site from where we watched dippers darting up and down the stream hunting for insects. The walk stays by the river in lodgepole and spruce forest broken by wet, flowery meadows for another 4 miles (6.4km) during which there are several easy fords. Then at Whiterock Creek, where there is a good campsite, the trail heads up to a low wooded saddle that marks the divide between the Two Medicine and Badger drainages. Dropping down into the latter the route passes the locked cabin of the Badger Guard Station around which camping is not permitted, although its porch makes a shady lunch spot. From here the North

Badger Trail is taken up a narrow valley hemmed in by the rocky slopes of Goat and Running Owl Mountains. Fords of Kip Creek and North Badger Creek are necessary and these required care when I was there. After the crossing of the latter, the trail switchbacks up steeply to a 6,250ft (1,875m) wooded saddle and then descends to the confluence of Elbow and Muskrat Creeks. The flat shelf of Lost Horse Camp is just above this junction and here we pitched our tent after a 17-mile (27-km) day. The site provides a good view down Muskrat Creek to Curly Bear Mountain.

Cold, early morning fords of both creeks serve to wake you up if you've stayed at Lost Horse Camp; they certainly did me! After a 4½ mile (7.2km) climb, Muskrat Pass at 6,000ft (1,800m) on the Continental Divide is reached, the Bob Marshall Wilderness entered and the Great Bear Wilderness, which lies on the far side of the pass, is touched upon for the only time. The gentle and pleasant, although mostly viewless, walking in dense forest continues for a while, but as the trail meanders on close to the Divide before crossing it again at 6,300ft (1,890m) Badger Pass and its extensive meadows, there opens up a view of rounded peaks. In early season, the trails here still have snow patches on them and are running with water. From the pass, there begins a slow descent of the Strawberry Creek valley, through alternating lodgepole pine and Engelmann's spruce forest. Small flower meadows break up the monotony of the trees and there are a number of creekside campsites, at one of which, 8 miles (12.8km) from Badger Pass, Scott and I stopped. The remnants of a huge log jam on the edge of the wide creek provided an idyllic spot for our kitchen and, as we lazed on the warm wood in the hot evening sun after dinner watching the cool, blue water rippling down between the dark borders of the forest, we were entertained by a sandpiper flitting up and down the pebble banks.

After another 3 miles (4.8km), Strawberry Creek has to be crossed. In mid-June this proved to be a hazardous crutch-deep ford and, as I hung on to the quivering ski pole out in the middle of the strong current, I thought that we really should have used the rope and it was with great relief that I reached the far shore, shivering from a combination of fear and cold. Luckily, an ascent follows and we were able to warm up quickly as we climbed to Sun River Pass, a densely wooded crossing of the Divide with no views. From here until Benchmark, the route lies in the Sun River Game Preserve, in which no hunting is allowed, as well as in the Bob Marshall Wilderness. The muddy trail undulates on through the trees to cross some meadows known as Round Park. Everywhere was very wet and at one point Scott actually had a shoe sucked off in an especially deep and glutinous bog. (We were walking in training shoes, ideal for the soft forest paths, but not so good for waterlogged and muddy areas.) There are meant to be good campsites in Round Park, but as the area was flooded Scott and I kept going to ascend beside Open Creek and camp in a small meadow with a good view of Signal Mountain. Again, this is a quiet, peaceful site where one can relax and unwind from the day's walk, the sort of wilderness camp which is very difficult to leave. Why make the effort of walking on when you could stay here in the sunshine watching the clouds pass overhead and the river running past as you lie under the shade of the trees?

From this point, over 50 miles (80km) from Marias Pass, the country starts to open up and the trail leaves the deep, forested river valleys and low-wooded ridges for more mountainous and rugged terrain. Glimpses of what is to come can be seen during the climb of Open Creek, as the headwall of the valley soaring up above pops in and out of view. The trail crosses the creek (the last water for 6 miles (9.6km)) and soon afterwards reaches open country below tiers of limestone cliffs. Suddenly the somewhat mysterious, confined atmosphere of the shady forest with its hints of hidden secrets and denizens is left behind and the world outside is revealed, as the vista expands from a few feet of trees and a shining strip of river to an open, unrestricted, airy spaciousness. With this comes a feeling of release, and Scott and I picked up speed without being aware of it as we hurried to partake of this new freedom. The gentle and relaxing mood engendered by the forest walking gave way to a rush of exhilaration as we headed for the heights.

Snowbanks lay across the trail as we wound our way up a minor wooded ridge that splits the cliffs to a wide snow basin, which would be a

*Scott Steiner below the Chinese Wall.*

flower meadow in just a few weeks' time. A steep climb, all on soft snow in mid-June, climbed by us in running shoes, but with ice axes, leads to the Divide and a fantastic view. Range upon range of snow-covered mountains fade away into the west, while to the south run the limestone terraces of the Bob Marshall Wilderness. Half a mile north along the Divide lies Kevan Mountain at 8,412ft (2,523m), well worth climbing if the weather is clear, as the view from the top is even better than that from the pass below, with the distant peaks of Glacier National Park to the north coming into view. Closer to hand is the green jewel of Lake Levale, visible below the cliffs to the south. The knowledge that one is deep in the wilderness here is confirmed by this view. There are no signs of humanity in any direction, even though one can see for mile after mile across the mountains and forests. The pervading sense is that this is a huge, untouched and pristine land, a land of natural grandeur, where the wildest of wildlife, the mighty grizzly bear and the wolf pack can roam free. May it remain so forever.

Scott and I spent an hour on the ridge despite a cold north wind, revelling in being high above the forests we'd walked through for so many days, before curving round to the north-west to 7,750ft (2,325m) Switchback Pass and the start of a 3,500ft (1,050m) descent back into the green blanket of the forest to the Spotted Bear River and Pentagon Guard Station 6 miles (9.6km) away. Four miles (6.4km) below the pass, a small creek provides the first water since Open Creek. The last part of this descent is on an excellent dry trail through dense forest broken by small meadows brilliant with flowers such as the scarlet Indian Paintbrush and the large yellow Mountain Mule's Ears. Several campsites are passed by as you descend. Mule deer were browsing in the forest round the wooden guard station and a yellow-haired porcupine stared at us from a bush beside

*The Chinese Wall.*

the trail. Beyond the cabin there are several fords, including two of Pentagon Creek and one of the Spotted Bear River, across which lies a good campsite where, 4 miles (6.4km) from the guard station and 14 miles (22.4km) from Open Creek, Scott and I camped, after a fulfilling and satisfying day that made up for all the previous days of slogging along muddy forest trails. It's my belief that you can only really appreciate the wilderness qualities of areas such as the Kevan Mountain Ridge if you've worked for them. To reach such areas easily, by motorised transport or after a short stroll from a car park, devalues them and reduces their glories to no more than picture-postcard tourist viewpoints.

A gradual climb for 6 miles (9.6km) in the Spotted Bear River valley, along a trail over-hung with thick spiny undergrowth (which lacerates your legs if you foolishly wear shorts as I did), leads to 6,200ft (1,860m) Spotted Bear Pass. Here, the appropriately named Wall

Trail is joined, appropriate because it heads straight for the scenic high point of the Bob Marshall Wilderness, the great limestone reef known as the Chinese Wall. However, after a mile I recommend leaving the Wall Trail, which cuts left to My Lake and a good, if well-used campsite, to follow the Continental Divide over 8,183ft (2,455m) Larch Hill, so-called because it's one of the few places in this region where the graceful alpine larch grows, to Larch Hill Pass where the Wall Trail is rejoined. The ascent to Larch Hill is quite steep, but well worth the effort for the views are superb, especially of the gradually unfolding Chinese Wall rippling away in waves of rock to the south. On my walk, this section was still completely covered in snow.

From the 7,700ft (2,310m) pass, the trail descends to the base of the Chinese Wall, which is then followed for several miles. Although over 20 miles (32km) from the nearest dirt road, the wall is a fairly popular destination, especially with horse parties, and many of the fragile timberline campsites along its base have been grossly abused. There may well be restrictions on camping in some areas, but, even if there aren't, great care should be taken not to add to the damage and, in particular, no fires should be lit. Too many of the small, slow growing timberline trees have already been cut down or stripped of branches for fires. We camped in the shelter of some scrubby trees near the source of Moose Creek with a good view of Cliff Mountain, after wandering for 4½ miles (7.2km) along the wall's base. The walk was exhilarating, although the snow-covered trail presented problems as we kept breaking through the snow and cutting and bruising our legs on boulders hidden under the crust. We soon found that climbing out of a knee-deep hole into soft snow with a heavy pack isn't easy. But the views made up for it, as above us towered the vertical, pale yellow cliff, while rolling away to the east from its base lay a succession of alpine cirques full of flowers divided from each other by long ridges that dropped down into the dark forest. Hawks, marmots and squirrels abound here.

A mule deer hung around our camp all night, a sure sign of a popular site. Then, early in the morning, we were woken by the sound of stonefall from the Chinese Wall. A steep climb leads from the site to the ridge at the base of Cliff Mountain and more views, before the trail starts to bend south-east and away from the Chinese Wall, as it begins a long descent of the West Fork of the South Fork of the Sun River. An excellent trail with a firm, dry surface makes for fast progress through the flower-filled meadows and woods and gives good views of the richly coloured rocks of the aptly-named Red Buttes. Just past the ford of Black Bear Creek, where we met three horse riders heading up to the Chinese Wall, Indian Point Guard Station is reached and you have a choice of routes. The (apparently) more scenic and less-

used route leads for 17 undulating miles (27.2km) to the roadhead at Benchmark. The more direct 11-mile (17.6-km) route stays by the West Fork of the South Fork and then the South Fork of the Sun River. This being our seventh day out from Marias Pass, Scott and I decided on the shorter route. Our supplies were dwindling and we had boxes of goodies waiting at Benchmark Wilderness Ranch.

I thought the direct route quite beautiful as it ran through wooded parkland, rich with flower meadows above the river. We camped 6 miles (9.6km) on from the Indian Point Guard Station, where the trail crosses the river on a bridge and turns up the South Fork towards Benchmark. From this site, it took us an hour and a half to reach the roadhead on a pleasant woodland trail. At Benchmark, there is a large campground designed for horse parties which we used. Here we encountered the large Connecticut Continental Divide Expedition group, a party of backpackers who were walking, as I was, all the way from Canada to Mexico. However, unlike my basically solo, unsupported trip (Scott was only with me for the first 500 miles), the CCDE had a back-up van transporting surplus gear and meeting them at roadheads with food supplies. Their numbers varied as people joined and left for different sections and only a few of them were going the whole way. Solo walkers usually progress faster than groups, so I was to leave the CCDE behind after 800 miles (1,280km) and not see them again. My own walk having been completed in late November I heard after I returned home that they'd finished in early January. Self-supporting or not, I wasn't averse to help when it was proffered, so Scott and I accepted the offer of a lift in the CCDE van down to the Wilderness Ranch to pick up our food boxes. The holding cost in 1985 was $20 per package. For another $1 you could have a cold shower (well, it's meant to be hot but it wasn't when I stood under it!) and cabins can also be rented.

Bud and Bev Heckman, who own the ranch, use it as the base for an outfitting business leading horse parties into the mountains, usually but not always for hunting purposes. Outfitters are found throughout the mountains of the western USA and Canada, usually operating in wilderness and unprotected forest service areas, as hunting is not allowed in national parks. They are the heirs to the first white trappers and frontiersmen and many, though not all of them, still tend to have a rather pioneering attitude to the wilderness. This can be somewhat at odds with no-trace backcountry ethics and a tension often exists between backpackers and horsepackers. It shouldn't be so, as the future for both activities lies in the preservation of the wilderness. Bud Heckman, looking every inch the western outdoorsman in his cowboy boots and hat, blue jeans and studded shirt, laughed at our description of hanging food to protect it against grizzlies. 'They won't trouble you round here,' he said, 'they're all too scared because this is a hunting area and even though they are a protected species they keep away from people and the sound of rifle shots.' Only in the national parks where hunting was banned, he went on, did grizzlies cause trouble. Yes, but *we're* not carrying high velocity rifles and travelling on horseback, we thought. Even so, we weren't as careful with our bear-avoidance techniques after leaving the ranch.

Back at the campground, we off-loaded our heavy and unnecessary rope, plus other surplus gear into the CCDE van and spent the rest of the day eating and relaxing. That night nighthawks (known as nightjars in Britain) screeched around the campground. A 10-mile (16-km) trek up the Straight Creek valley leads from Benchmark to the Green Fork Guard Station and 3 miles (4.8km) into this walk, the Scapegoat Wilderness is entered. Beyond the guard station, where we had lunch and watched a hummingbird speeding about like a giant manic bee, a vast burnt area is crossed, with young lodgepoles rapidly covering the scars, as the trail ascends Green Fork, while above the forest rises the rocky summit of Halfmoon Peak. Two and a half miles (4km) past the

*Forest camp in the Bob Marshall Wilderness.*

*The author on the Continental Divide with Caribou Peak in the background, Scapegoat Wilderness.*

guard station, a cliff can be seen out of which gushes a spring, and, down other high crags nearby, waterfalls tumble. Soon afterwards, the wooded saddle between Scapegoat Mountain and Halfmoon Peak is crossed and the trail descends into the flat basin of Halfmoon Park, below a gently curving 1,000ft (300m) lime-stone wall. To the south, the cliffs are topped by the 9,200ft (2,760m) summit of Scapegoat Mountain. This amphitheatre is an excellent place for a scenic camp, although when I was there the mosquitoes were out in force. At 6,950ft (2,085m) this is one of the highest sites on the walk.

Dawn revealed a cold grey headwall that slowly turned to burnished gold as the sun rose. I felt reluctant to leave Halfmoon Park and kept turning round for a final look at the cliffs, as the trail descended through meadows beside Halfmoon Creek. After 1½ miles (2.4km) the trail crosses the creek and turns up beside Telephone Creek to the Dearborn River which is followed downstream for just ½ mile (0.8km) to a junction with the Cave Creek Trail. This is taken upwards for 1,400ft (420m) to the Continental Divide and magnificent views dominated by the sheer cliffs of Scapegoat Mountain to the northwest. Here, for the first time, there begins a ridge walk along the Divide. The narrow crest is rocky and flower-strewn and so enjoyable to walk along that Scott and I, oblivious of where we were, walked off it in the wrong direction! We only realised what we'd done when the descent began to 'feel' wrong, an indefinable growing sense of uneasiness that I find comes over me when I've made a navigational error. In fact, we'd turned down the Lost Cabin Creek Trail which met the Dearborn River Trail 4 miles (6.4km) upstream of where we'd intended to join it. Once we'd realized our mistake, it was easier to go on than turn back.

However, the route as described by Jim Wolf in his guidebook seems to involve a fair amount of uncertainty and bushwhacking, so the Lost Cabin Creek Trail may well be a good way to go. Both routes are about the same length at 10 miles (16km) or so. A mile and a half (2.4km) further along the Dearborn River from where the two trails meet up, there are several campsites in the wide valley near where the river is split by several large shingle banks. As a steep climb comes next, this is a good place to stop. This is exactly what Scott and I did, camping in a tree grove not far from four of the CCDE group.

The 1,700ft (510m) in 2 miles (3.2km) ascent up the Blacktail Creek Trail from the Dearborn River leads back to the Continental Divide and a long walk along, or just below, its winding ridge, much of it cross-country. Some careful navigation with map and compass is needed in the wooded sections, especially at the viewless saddles, to make sure a spur ridge is not followed by mistake. Most of the walking, however, is above the trees on gravel and grass with flowers all around and wonderful views of the Scapegoat Wilderness. After 5 miles (8km) there are views down to blue-green Bighorn Lake and the Valley of the Moon below the loose shaley slopes of Caribou Peak. The route avoids those slopes by cutting down into the Valley of the Moon on a good path. There is water and a good campsite here but Scott and I wanted to camp further on upon the Divide itself, so we loaded up here with 3

gallons of water, with none certain for the next and last 19 miles (30.4km) of the walk, and commenced the climb back up above timberline. The Divide is reached after 1¾ miles (2.8km) and the Scapegoat Wilderness left after 1¼ (2km) more. A partially wooded 8,150ft (2,445m) unnamed summit with a steep drop-off to the east and vast views in every direction 2 miles (3.2km) beyond the Wilderness boundary, is where we bivvied out. Sturdy 10 to 15ft (4.5m) high whitebark pine provided shelter from the wind. Clarks Nutcrackers screeched around the hilltop and prairie falcons soared in the air above as we laid out our sleeping bags on the soft turf. A pleasant pale sunset ended a fine day.

From the 8,150ft (2,445m) summit, a complex route along the grassy Divide leads to 6,323ft (1,897m) Lewis and Clark Pass. Here, returning from the two men's epic expedition across the continent in 1804-6, Meriweather Lewis recrossed the Continental Divide on his way back east on 7 July 1806. South of the pass, our meandering route climbs Green Mountain, at 7,453ft (2,236m) and then travels on jeep roads and cross-country for the last 5½ miles (8.8km) to Rogers Pass and Montana Highway 200. The final drop to the 5,600 ft (1,680m) pass is very steep.

The daily Great Falls – Kalispell bus service runs through the pass, but on the day we arrived no bus came (we later learnt that the drivers were on strike) and we had to wait over four hours for a lift. As it was very hot and we'd had no water since the 3 gallons we'd picked up in the Valley of the Moon, which had long been finished, this was a most unpleasant and thirsty wait. During it I reflected on the fact that in January 1954 the temperature here fell to −70°F, a record for the USA. And with those cold thoughts, we leave the lonely wildernesses of the northern Montana Rockies.

# THE ROUTE

| MILEAGE/(KM) | | PLACE | ELEVATION | |
|---|---|---|---|---|
| | | | ft | m |
| 0.0 | 0.0 | Elk Calf Trail | 5,215 | 1,564.5 |
| 4.1 | 6.5 | Trail 101 | 5,050 | 1,515 |
| 14.5 | 23.2 | Badger Guard Station | 5,500 | 1,650 |
| 20.0 | 32.0 | North Badger Creek | 5,750 | 1,725 |
| 23.1 | 36.9 | Lost Horse Camp | 5,500 | 1,650 |
| 26.7 | 42.7 | Muskrat Pass | 6,000 | 1,800 |
| 29.0 | 46.4 | Badger Pass/Bob Marshall Wilderness | 6,300 | 1,890 |
| 40.2 | 64.3 | Strawberry Creek final ford | 5,350 | 1,605 |
| 45.2 | 72.3 | Sun River Pass | 6,300 | 1,890 |
| 56.3 | 90.0 | Pass south of Kevan Mountain | 8,050 | 2,415 |
| 63.1 | 100.9 | Pentagon Guard Station | 4,850 | 1,455 |
| 73.4 | 117.4 | Spotted Bear Pass | 6,700 | 2,010 |
| 75.2 | 120.3 | Larch Hill | 8,183 | 2,454.9 |
| 81.6 | 130.5 | Saddle below Cliff Mountain | 7,600 | 2,280 |
| 84.7 | 135.5 | West Fork of South Fork, Sun River | 6,050 | 1,815 |
| 90.5 | 144.8 | Indian Point Guard Station | 5,400 | 1,620 |
| 101.5 | 162.4 | Benchmark | 5,300 | 1,590 |
| 111.3 | 178.0 | Green Fork Guard Station | 6,000 | 2,277 |
| 115.0 | 184.0 | Halfmoon Park | 6,950 | 2,085 |
| 120.5 | 192.8 | Continental Divide east of Scapegoat Mountain | 7,800 | 2,340 |
| 134.1 | 214.5 | Blacktail Creek Trail junction | 5,250 | 1,575 |
| 142.4 | 227.8 | Valley of the Moon | 7,700 | 2,310 |
| 154.9 | 247.8 | Lewis and Clark Pass | 6,400 | 1,920 |
| 161.8 | 258.8 | Rogers Pass | 5,600 | 1,680 |

From the Summit Campground at Marias Pass on Highway 2, take the **Elk Calf Trail** (5,215ft, Mile 0) for 4 miles to a junction with **Trail 101** (5,050ft, Mile 4.1), a dirt road at this point, which is followed southwards besides the South Fork of the Two Medicine River, which is crossed several times. The river is left for an ascending trail (still 101) at Whiterock Creek (5,750ft, Mile 12.5) that leads over a wooded divide and down to the **Badger Guard Station** (5,500, Mile 14.5). Trail 101 is left here for a dirt road that soon becomes the North Badger Trail (No 103), which is followed up the North Badger Creek valley to a Junction in a meadow, where it is left for the Elbow Creek Trail (No 145), just before **North Badger Creek** is crossed (5,750ft, Mile 20),

which leads to the junction of Elbow Creek and Muskrat Creek at **Lost Horse Camp** (5,500ft, Mile 23.1). From the camp, take the Muskrat Creek Trail (No 147) which crosses both creeks and then ascends above Muskrat Creek to **Muskrat Pass** (6,000ft, Mile 26.7). Here the Bob Marshall Wilderness is entered and the trail meanders along the Continental Divide to **Badger Pass** (6,300ft Mile 29). From the pass, take the Strawberry Creek Trail (No 161) down the **Strawberry Creek** valley, crossing the creek several times to a final **ford** (5,350ft, Mile 40.2), beyond which the trail ascends beside Bowl Creek to **Sun River Pass** (6,300ft, Mile 45.2) on the Bowl Creek (No 324) and Sun River Pass (No 116) Trails. After 3 more miles, take the

Open Creek Trail to Round Park and up beside Open Creek to where the Wall Trail (No 175) joins from the left and is taken up to the high pass on the Divide south of **Kevan Mountain** (8,050ft, Mile 56.3). Descend ¾ mile to Switchback Pass where the Basin Creek– Pentagon Cabin Trail (No 177) is taken, for a long switchbacking descent to the Spotted Bear River and the **Pentagon Guard Station** (4,850ft, Mile 63.1). Here the Spotted Bear River Trail (No 83) is taken across Pentagon Creek and for the 10-mile climb to **Spotted Bear Pass** (6,700ft, Mile 73.4). The Wall Trail (No 175) is rejoined for a mile to a junction with a trail which is taken over **Larch Hill** (8,183ft, Mile 75.2) to Larch Hill Pass and the north end of the Chinese Wall. The Wall Trail is joined again ¼ mile beyond the pass and followed along the base of the Chinese Wall to a saddle near the base of **Cliff Mountain** (7,600ft, Mile 81.6). Here, the trail leaves the wall and heads south and east to the **West Fork of the South Fork of the Sun River** (6,050ft, Mile 84.7), which is followed to the **Indian Point Guard Station** (5,400ft, Mile 90.5). The well-used trail continues beside the West Fork and then the South Fork to the roadhead and campground at **Benchmark** (5,300ft, Mile 101.5). Follow the road for ½ mile to the Straight Creek Trail (No 112), which is taken into the Scapegoat Wilderness (5,600ft, Mile 104.7) and on to the **Green Fork Guard Station** (6,000ft, Mile 112.1). Here the Green Fork Trail (No 228) is joined and followed up to **Halfmoon Park** (6,950ft, Mile 116) and the Halfmoon Trail (No 216) which leads to the Dearborn River and then a junction with the Cave Creek Trail (No 217) (6,450ft, Mile 118.8). Follow the latter trail up to the **Continental Divide** (7,800ft, Mile 121.3), south-east of Scapegoat Mountain. Travel along the Divide for 2½ miles on an intermittent trail to a junction with the Lost Cabin Creek Trail, which is taken for the 3 mile descent to the Dearborn

River. Five and a half miles down the river leave the trail along its banks for the **Blacktail Creek Trail** (No 207) (5,250ft, Mile 134.1) and a climb back up to the Divide which is followed, with a few contours below it, cross-country for 6 miles to a trail that descends into the **Valley of the Moon** (7,700ft, Mile 142.4). Ascend south-south-east back to the Divide near Caribou Peak and again follow the Divide, mostly cross-country, to **Lewis and Clark Pass** (6,400ft, Mile 154.9) taking care not to take a wrong turning on the wooded saddles. Jeep tracks, dirt roads, pack trail and bits of cross-country then lead over Green Mountain, and finally, down steeply to **Rogers Pass** and Highway 200 (5,600ft, Mile 161.8).

## MAPS

USGS 1:24,000 topographic maps: Summit; Hyde Creek; Crescent Cliff; Morningstar Mountain; Gooseberry Park; Pentagon Mountain; Porphyry Reef; Trilobite Peak; Bungalow Mountain; Three Sisters; Slategoat Mountain; Amphitheatre Mountain; Prairie Reef; Trap Mountain; Benchmark; Wood Lake; Scapegoat Mountain; Jakie Creek; Steamboat Mountain; Heart Lake; Caribou Peak; Blowout Mountain; Cadette Creek; Roger's Pass. Only the last eight of these are essential as they cover the final cross-country section. For the earlier part of the walk, the Forest Service Teton Ranger District Map 3, Bob Marshall Wilderness and Scapegoat Wilderness maps are adequate.

## RECOMMENDED GUIDEBOOK

*Guide to the Continental Divide Trail Volume 1: Northern Montana* by James R. Wolf (Continental Divide Trail Society).

# The North Cascades:
## Snoqualmie Pass to Manning Park   256 miles (409.6km)

*Climbing the steep ridge below Shuksan*
*clumps of pine*
*float out of the fog*

Gary Snyder   *Riprap and Cold Mountain Poems*

This is arguably the toughest, most serious and intimidating walk in the book. It's the longest route, although only by 20 miles (32km) and it undoubtedly involves far more ascent than any of the others, with many long, steep climbs. It also takes place in the area with the worst weather, as heavy rain and snow can be expected at any time, although the winter snows don't usually start until October. Only in the last 70 miles (112km) where the route lies on the eastern side of the Cascades, in the rainshadow of the higher peaks of Mount Baker, Mount Shuksan and the Picket Range to the west, can sunny weather be expected, but it should not be relied upon. Many of the creeks and rivers are not bridged and fords can be dangerous. The higher sections of the route may only be snow-free for six weeks of the year,

*The North Cascades from Fire Creek Pass.*

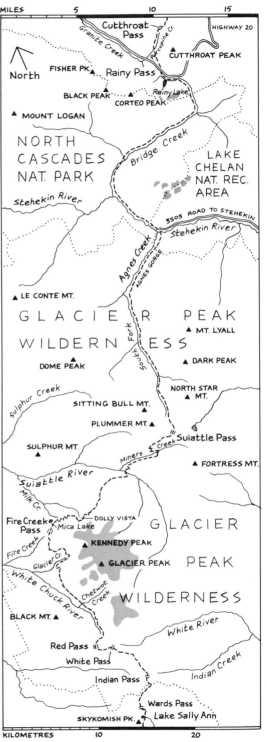

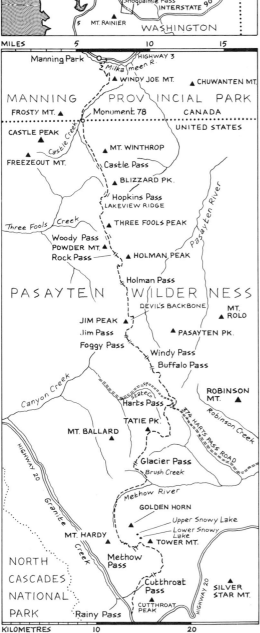

from late July to mid-September. Much of the trail winds round steep avalanche slopes and would be either highly dangerous or just about impassable in deep snow. Avalanches are common. Above timberline, the trail is very exposed to any storms and there are no easy escape routes. When it's not raining or snowing, the mosquitos and biting flies can be a real problem.

There is only one supply point on the route, at Stevens Pass after 70 miles (112km) and the amenities here (café, gas station and ski area) are limited. The ranger station might hold parcels for hikers. To find out, write to the Skykomish Ranger District Headquarters, Skykomish, WA 98288. However, after 168 miles (268.8km), there is a roadhead from where a bus can be caught to the small resort of Stehekin on Lake Chelan where there are better facilities, including a post office. Even if both these supply points are used, heavy packs will be inevitable. Two to three weeks will be needed for the walk.

Given all these disadvantages, why should anyone undertake this walk? The answer is, because on the one hand it is a challenge; you *do* have to cope with a real wilderness, and on the other because the North Cascades are some of the most rugged and impressive mountains anywhere, an alpine range of sheer-sided rocky peaks packed together tightly above myriad deep glacier-carved canyons and laced with an incredible 756 glaciers, the largest number in the USA outside Alaska. The trail is tough because it traverses the heart of this savage landscape, swooping down into the depths of the forest from high mountain passes, then climbing straight back up past timberline lakes and cirques to the next pass before descending again, a glorious walk for any experienced backpacker who is a lover of mountain scenery.

The route, the northernmost section of the Pacific Crest Trail, starts at Snoqualmie Pass on Interstate 90 where there is a campground,

store and post office as well as a ski resort, and finishes in Canada's Manning Park on Highway 3, where again there are facilities. Buses can be caught to and from both ends of the trail. During its traverse of the North Cascades, the route crosses the protected areas of the Alpine Lakes Wilderness, the Glacier Peak Wilderness, the Lake Chelan National Recreation Area, the North Cascades National Park, the Pasayten Wilderness and Manning Park. Permits are needed and can be obtained from the Mount Baker–Snoqualmie National Forest, 1601 Second Avenue Building, Seattle, WA 98101 for the first part of the walk and from the Supervisor's Office, Okanagan National Forest, PO Box 950, Okanagan, WA 98840 for the Pasayten Wilderness. The route finishes by crossing into Canada, providing a link, although not in a direct way, with the next three walks. Through-walkers should contact the Canadian authorities for advice about the border crossing.

In keeping with the weather pattern of the area, I spent my first intended day on the trail at Snoqualmie Pass in heavy rain and thick mist with snow forecast for above 6,500ft (1,950m). The date was 9 September. The rain continued all night and into the next day. By 3pm I was so frustrated that I decided to start the walk anyway. There's not much to do at Snoqualmie Pass in the rain! The clouds had lifted enough to show a dusting of new snow on the higher slopes. From the trailhead just off Interstate 90, the trail starts to climb immediately up several switchbacks, a foretaste of the many ascents to come, and enters the Alpine Lakes Wilderness. Two backpackers I met descending (retreating, they said!) told me there was snow on the trail higher up and sure enough on reaching 5,000ft (1,500m) after 4 or so miles (6.4km) of ascent I found a couple

*(Preceding pages) Lake Valhalla and Lichtenberg Mountain.*

of inches of fresh snow on the trail which, as it lay on top of wet mud, made the going very slippery. Despite the thick clouds shrouding the peaks, I found the trail, which clings tenuously to steep, rocky hillsides that fall away into deep valleys, very dramatic. In places, narrow ledges have been blasted into the rock to allow the walker passage. During the airy crossing of these snowy terraces I was glad I was carrying an ice axe. After 7 miles (11.2km) a wide 5,280ft (1,584m) high pass is reached with Ridge and Gravel Lakes either side of it.

I camped on bare ground near the latter lake and quickly zipped myself into the tent as a steady drizzle fell. The temperature was 8°C (46°F) but it felt much colder. By 7am it had fallen to 4°C (40°F) and soft, wet snow covered the tent. Puddles had formed under the groundsheet and all around the tent and everything inside was damp. At least, I thought, it hadn't frozen overnight, something I'd feared as it would have made the trail really treacherous. By 9am the snow was melting and heavy rain was falling. My journal sums up the next 14 miles of walking: 'a wet, wet day'. Even though I wore full waterproofs, the air was so humid I was soon soaked to the skin. Even the best 'breathable' Gore-tex fabric couldn't push body moisture out into such a saturated atmosphere. Above 5,000ft (1,500m) the snow lay up to 6in (15cm) deep on the trail so my feet were also soaked. In the lower areas, the trail ran with water. For 4 miles (6.4km) from Gravel Lake the trail is so narrow and on such steep slopes that a sign warns horse parties that there are no places they can leave it. According to the guidebook, water may be scarce for nearly 8 miles (12.8km) from the lake. This was not a problem when I was there!

From the few glimpses I caught of the scenery it looked magnificent, but all I saw most of the time was mud, snow and swirling cloud. However, in clear weather this should be a superb walk as the trail passes above many deep lake basins as it crosses the slopes of Alaska and Huckleberry Mountains to the steep-sided notch of Needle Site Gap. After traversing along Chikamin Ridge to a high point of 5,760ft (1,728m) the trail drops down into the Park Lakes basin where there are campsites, although camping isn't allowed by the lakes themselves. A short climb leads to a saddle, after which there is a seemingly interminable (at least in torrential rain) descent down sixty-six switchbacks to Lemah Creek at just 3200ft (960m) above sea level. I camped by the creek, a foaming torrent after all the rain, on a very wet site.

At 3am I was woken by a small animal, probably a chipmunk, sneaking into the tent and stealing some trail mix. The rain had stopped and a few stars sparkled in the sky. The foot of my sleeping bag was damp as a pool of water had formed at the end of the tent. The morning brought more rain but the wet weather was slowly clearing as I undertook the long, slow 2,300ft (690m) forested climb up Escon-

dido Ridge and the ascent gave good views across the Lemah valley to the steep slopes and hanging glaciers of cloud-wrapped Lemah Peak. Two rifle shots rang out from somewhere close ahead as I climbed higher, so I started to whistle and sing, not wanting to be mistaken for a deer. Two men holding rifles at the ready came round a bend in the trail 'Seen anything moving?' asked one. I didn't like the sound of that 'anything'. The hunting season, it turned out, had begun the day before (11 September).

The trail finally emerges in a pleasant rocky cirque graced with a small pool. Here I found two other walkers, Jay and Robert, with all their gear spread out to dry on the now sun-warmed rocks. My own belongings soon joined theirs and the cirque took on the appearance of an outdoor jumble sale with well-used gear, faded in colour, strewn everywhere. The trail continues across the upper part of Escondido Ridge past a number of campsites. Far below lies the dark slash of Escondido Lake while across the Waptus valley and the larger dark-

*Janice Cabin, the only backcountry shelter on the trail.*

*Mount Daniel.*

ness of Waptus Lake lies a panorama of snow-capped peaks, upon one of which a huge gently-angled rock slab, at least 1,000ft (300m) long, reaches up almost to the summit. From the ridge more endless switchbacks lead down to 3,040ft (912m) and the bridged Waptus River. There are many campsites here and more by Waptus Lake which lies not far away. I camped by the river.

Two and a half miles (4km) and 350ft (105m) of ascent from the Waptus River, there is a junction with the Spinola Creek Trail. Ten miles (16km) away down this trail and the Waptus River Trail, lies the Salmon La Sac Guard Station and a roadhead and camp-grounds, so this could be a quick way out of the mountains if one were needed. Our trail continues upwards through open forest laced with avalanche chutes that give many excellent views of the rock tower of Cathedral Peak at 6,724ft (2,017m) before reaching an unnamed pass and descending slowly to Spinola Creek

and Deep Lake at 4,390ft (1,317m). The next 3 miles (4.8km) consist of a steep ascent for 1,300ft (390m) to Cathedral Pass, but the views are so good during the upper half of the climb that there are plenty of excuses to stop.

From the pass, a dipping and rising traverse across the glaciated slopes of the massive 7,899ft (2,369.7m) Mount Daniel leads to 4,450ft (1,335m) Deception Pass 5 miles (8km) further on. A notice on the trail suggests that one should detour to avoid a dangerous stream crossing 3½ miles (5.6km) beyond Cathedral Pass, but hikers I met walking south told me to ignore this notice as the stream was easily crossed on logs. This may not always be so, of course. High above the trail are waterfalls and hanging valleys but Mount Daniel is not seen in full until Deception Pass is reached. A wooded traverse leads from the pass for 3½ miles (5.6km) past 17 Mile Camp to Deception Lakes where there is a choice of routes. The PCT runs for 3½ miles (5.6km) to Glacier

Lake via Pieper Pass, while the old, unmaintained Cascade Crest Trail takes a 1½ mile (2.4km) shorter route via Surprise Gap to the lake. I took the latter route and was glad I did, as Surprise Gap lived up to its name. From the rough, steep, decaying path to the gap there were good views back to Mac Peak but the real reward for the climb was the superb view of distant shining 10,541ft (3,162.3m) Glacier Peak over Glacier Lake that suddenly appears. At Glacier Lake there is meant to be a lean-to shelter big enough for six people but I failed to find it and camped by the lake.

Trap Pass at 5,800ft (1.740m) is reached after 2½ miles (4km) and an 800ft (240m) climb from Glacier Lake. After dropping 180ft (54m) to Trap Lake, the trail traverses above timberline to give good views of the towering, curved rock spire of Thunder Mountain before starting a long 11 mile (17.6km) undulating meander through slowly declining hills, past many small lakes and potential campsites to a final steeper descent below ski lifts to 4060ft (1218m) Steven's Pass and Highway 2, 70 miles (112km) from Snoqualmie Pass. A gas station and cafè, which have seasonal opening hours, lie on the pass a short distance from where the trail crosses it, these were closed on 14 September. The nearest towns are Skykomish 16 miles (25.6km) to the west, and Leavenworth, 36 miles (57.6km) to the east. I crossed straight over the road and headed back into the forest.

There are good campsites by Nason Creek, which the trail follows for a mile (1.6km) just 2½ miles (4km) from the pass but I went on, intent on reaching a shelter cabin another 7 miles (11.2km) along the trail. *En route* the trail climbs to a 5,030ft (1,509m) saddle from where beautiful Lake Valhalla can be seen under the towering cliffs of the west face of

*Autumn colours along the Pacific Crest Trail.*

5,844ft (1,753m) Lichtenberg Mountain. The descent from the saddle passes within 200yds (180m) of the lake. The rest of the route to the dilapidated, open-fronted Janice Cabin and shallow Lake Janus is in dense forest. Here I met up again with Jay J. Johnson (first encountered in Chapter 4) and also an Australian hiker named Ron Ellis, who I'd been mistaken for several times, Americans assuring me that our accents were identical. The cabin abounds with bold mice, so it's necessary to hang all food from the rafters.

The trail beyond the cabin passes through meadows and over ridges with ever-more spectacular views of Glacier Peak, an all-white giant floating above the dark forest. There are many possible campsites, the one by Pear Lake, 9 miles (14.4km) from Janice Cabin, among granite boulders, is particularly appealing. On the climb from the lake to 5,250ft (1,575m) Frozen Finger Gap the reason for its name becomes apparent. Farther back can be seen the peaks around Snoqualmie Pass and then way to the south the big white hazy mass of Mount Rainier. More ridges are crossed before Pass Creek, where there is a campsite, is reached and shortly afterwards Cady Pass, at 4,310ft (1,293m). Here, a 1,200ft (360m) ascent leads in 2 miles (3.2km) to the shoulder of 6,368ft (1,910m) Skykomish Peak. In mid-September the slopes of this peak are rich with delicious blueberries and Ron Ellis and I found our pace slowed considerably as we kept stopping to eat handfuls of them on the contour round the peak. It was late evening when we finally descended to pretty timberline Lake Sally Ann at 5,479ft (1,643.7m) and a fine campsite on a nearby flat-topped ridge. This site is popular and we found Jay and two other hikers already there.

A sharp north-east wind, totally clear sky and beautiful dawn light at Lake Sally Ann promised a good day for the above-timberline walk into the heart of the Glacier Peak Wilder-

ness. Purple and red berry bushes lined the trail as it crossed the autumn-coloured treeless hillsides towards the searing white mountain of ice that is Glacier Peak. From Lake Sally Ann, the trail climbs to Ward Pass (5,710ft/1,713m) and then follows a ridge for 2½ miles (4km) to the southern boundary of the Glacier Peak Wilderness on the side of Kodak Peak (6,121ft/1,836m). Glacier Peak dominates the view, but all around are other rugged peaks white with snowfields. A descent leads to 5,020ft (1,506m) Indian Pass from where, as is usual in this area, the trail immediately starts to climb again, reaching 5,904ft (2,223m) White Pass after 4 miles (6.4km) and then 6,500ft (1,950m) Red Pass after another 2 miles (3.2km). The latter pass gives perhaps the best view of the walk with the stunning vista of the 5 miles (8km) distant Glacier Peak, straight ahead over the deep snow fields of the White Chuck River canyon.

The descent from Red Pass is usually snowbound, although it wasn't when I was there. If it is, the recommended ploy is to slide straight down the snow into the White Chuck River valley and then head downstream until the trail is regained. The trail proper descends more sedately for 3 miles (4.8km) past numerous campsites to cross the river on a bridge 2,500ft (750m) below the pass. I found myself most reluctant to leave the bare glaciated valley and plunge back into the dense claustrophobic woods here. Six and a half miles (10.4km) of trail leads in and out of the forest and across many roaring glacier-fed creeks along the lower western slopes of Glacier Peak before climbing up to 5,640ft (1,692m) and Glacier Creek, where there is a superbly situated campsite. Note, however, that the site is in an avalanche chute. I camped here anyway, revelling in the views up the canyon to the icefields of Glacier Peak.

The switchbacking trail continues up and down over more ridges before, 3½ miles

(5.6km) from Glacier Creek, it climbs for 1,000ft (300m) to 6,350ft (1,905m) Fire Creek Pass, another superlative viewpoint looking out on the rugged heart of the North Cascades. To the south and west towers Glacier Peak. A mile (1.6km) long 900ft (270m) descent leads down to a superb cirque containing lovely Mica Lake which is always at least partially covered with ice. There follows a knee-jarring, bone-shaking 1,600ft (480m) descent down to glacial Milk Creek whose bridge was destroyed in 1982, probably by an avalanche. The unremitting plunge into the valley is made worse by the sight throughout of the trail switchbacking for 1,900ft (570m) and 2½ miles (4km) up the far wall of the canyon, an ascent that starts as soon as Milk Creek is crossed. The hot, fly-ridden ascent took me 1¼ hours. It seemed longer. The trail here runs east along the northern flanks of Glacier Peak. Once the ridgetop is reached, more stupendous views open out with the Suiattle River visible far below. Away to the north-west can be seen the tiny white cone of Mount Baker, the northernmost of the Cascade strato-volcanoes.

After 2 miles (3.2km) of gentle ridge wandering, a relief after all the punishing steep ascents and descents, the rollercoaster is resumed with a fifty-nine switchback 3,100ft (930m) descent all the way down to Vista Creek at 2,877ft (863m). Near the top of this . drop lies Dolly Vista campsite in a superb situation. I passed this by with regret and camped 7½ miles (12km) further on deep in the forest by Miners Creek, near the Suiattle River, surrounded by massive Douglas firs. I chose Miners Creek to camp by, because the water was clear, rather than grey with glacier silt, like that of the Suiattle River. Nearby at Lyman Camp two hunters with horses were ensconced round a roaring fire. The 22-mile (35.2km) day from Glacier Creek had been long and tiring, so I was soon in my sleeping bag reading by candlelight, to be disturbed soon

*Trail sign at Cutthroat Pass.*

afterwards by a hunter who poked his rifle through the tent door. 'Seen any other hunters?' he asked. Once I'd recovered from the shock of having a gun pointed at me unexpectedly, I directed him to Lyman Camp.

A small mouse hurtled round the tent, exploring all my belongings, particularly my dirty socks, undisturbed by my presence. I chased it out, then hung my food from a tree branch feeling sure that the mouse would be back, and it was, waking me up in the middle of the night by trying to remove a strand of my hair! I expelled it, then zipped the tent firmly shut and went back to sleep.

The severity of the trail begins to lessen once the Suiattle River is crossed, although the walker could be forgiven for doubting that this is so during the 3,000ft (900m) climb to 5,983ft (1,795m) Suiattle Pass. However, a

*Ron Ellis at Red Pass with Glacier Peak in the background.*

look at the map reveals that the next 25 miles (40km) is mostly downhill along the South Fork Agnes Creek. Initially, the climb to the pass ascends to Middle Ridge which is followed to a good campsite by Miners Creek and the rest of the ascent. Glacier Peak dominates the view to the south, but from the pass, the eye is pulled northwards to the rugged face of Fortress Mountain and the peaks around the South Fork. *En route* to the creek, the trail rounds two impressive rock-walled cirques below Plummer and Sitting Bull Mountains. Shortly after arriving at the creek, Hemlock Camp, a large site with benches, table and fire rings, is reached. Other well-used sites occur as the trail descends into the deepening canyon. There is one view down into the gorge the creek has carved just before it joins the West Fork. Then, 11½ miles (18.4km) from Suiattle Pass, and, at an elevation of only 2,160ft (648m) the trail reaches the last campsite before the Glacier Peak Wilderness is left behind. Here at Five Mile Camp

I had a surprise reunion. Familiar sounding voices had me hurrying the last few yards to the site. Two startled faces turned towards me and then voices called out in welcome as I greeted two trail companions I hadn't seen for three months.

Four months earlier I'd travelled through the snowbound High Sierras on the John Muir Trail (see pages 10–25) with three American backpackers. I knew Larry Lake was way ahead, but I'd been hoping to catch up with Scott Steiner and Dave Rehbehn before I finished the walk, as I knew from the trail registers that I was walking further each day than them. They were only ahead because they'd skipped a section of a few hundred miles, not having time for the whole trail. I'd made many calculations as to when I'd see them again, but as with most of my attempts at arithmetic they were wrong and I hadn't expected to meet them for several more days, if at all. They hadn't expected to see me either and were astonished when I

*Cutthroat Pass.*

*Methow Pass and Mount Hardy.*

walked into their camp. That night we sat up late swapping stories – we all had many to tell.

Continuing down the canyon, the trail reaches the Stehekin River Road after 5 miles (8km) (hence the name of the camp). A few hundred yards down the road is the High Bridge Ranger Station from where shuttle buses run to the little resort of Stehekin on the banks of Lake Chelan. The journey takes about an hour. There is a campground near the ranger station if you miss the bus on the day you arrive there. Stehekin provides supplies, meals, lodgings, and a National Park Information Centre where you can obtain wilderness permits. There is also a post office, where I picked up a supply parcel and a bundle of mail. One of the letters had been posted in England just six days previously! Purple Point Campground, where I stayed, is ¼ mile (0.4km) north of the town. Black bears can be a problem here, so it's important to hang up your food.

As it's the only supply point easily accessible from the trail and well worth a visit in itself, Stehekin is a recommended detour. Snoqualmie Pass is a long 168 miles (268.8km) behind you here, but there are still 88 miles (140.8km) to go and most walkers will want a break before completing the trail. Stehekin and the Lake Chelan National Recreation Area can only be reached by ferry or float-plane. The lake is 50 miles (80km) long and reaches a depth of 1,586ft (475.8m), 488ft (146.5m) below sea level. If you want to finish the walk at Stehekin the ferry can be caught to the city of Chelan at the far end of the lake.

After half a day spent relaxing in Stehekin's café and watching the float-planes arriving and departing, we returned to Agnes Creek by the shuttle bus to spend a night in the shelter at the High Bridge Campground. I wanted to reach Manning Park in four days rather than the week the others were planning on, so I left them behind on the long gradual wooded ascent of Bridge Creek that takes the walker

into the North Cascades National Park and, after 19 miles (30.4km), to the North Cascades Highway at Rainy Pass, where there are toilets at the trailhead, but no other facilities.

It was on this trail that I met the bear. As I pushed on, keen to climb out of the trees, I rounded a large bush and was shocked into stopping. Thirty feet (9m) away, a large, really black, black bear was walking towards me. It too stopped and, for a few seconds which felt like hours, we stared at each other. Then the bear rushed away uphill at a rate that made me realize just why running away from a bear is pointless. Feeling exhilarated by the encounter, I strode on and crossed the highway to camp after another 1½ miles (2.4km) by Porcupine Creek after 21 miles (33.6km) and 3,500ft (1,050m) of ascent.

The ascent back into the mountains continues beyond the creek for the 3½ miles (5.6km) and 1,800ft (540m) of elevation that leads to 6,820ft (2,046m) Cutthroat Pass. The upper part of the trail to the pass switchbacks up the steep glaciated cirque wall of the headwaters of Porcupine Creek. Tamaracks or alpine larches decorate the route here, their needles a golden yellow in mid-September emphasizing the end of summer along with the reds and yellows of the fading foliage of the many bushes and shrubs that line the trail. These colours are amplified by the yellow Golden Horn granodiorite rock that prevails in this region. We are back, after the brief diversion to Lake Chelan, in the rugged scenery of the North Cascades with rocky peaks rising all around. From the pass, the trail curves round two cirques on steep scree below sheer cliffs and with good views of the peaks across the valley below especially the tapered wedge of Tower Mountain.

Next comes a traverse above the glacial valley of Swamp Creek, with superb views to Methow Pass still more than 5 miles (8km) of walking away, that leads down to 6,290ft (1,887m) Granite Pass where there is a campsite. A further traverse across the open lower slopes of Tower Mountain leads to a meadow in a bowl below Snowy Lakes and some idyllic campsites. Methow Pass, at 6,600ft (1,980m) lies above the bowl and is soon reached. Again, rock peaks tower all around with Mount Hardy (7,197ft/2,159m) and Golden Horn (8,366ft/ 2,510m) drawing us on ahead. So down we go to the West Fork Methow River at 4,390ft (1,317m) which is followed for nearly 4 miles (6.4km) before starting the 2,600ft (780m) climb up beside Brush Creek to Glacier Pass, then another unnamed pass at 6,900ft (2,070m). I camped a mile (1.6km) before this pass by a tiny trickling creek among alpine larch and subalpine fir just below Tatie Peak at 7,386ft (2,218m). The day had been cool but sunny and I felt very contented as I sat watching a thin crescent moon rising into the darkening sky.

Dawn brought a light frost, very heavy dew and a cold east wind. The high level traversing trail continues over several passes, a timberline route broken by the gravel mine road at 6,198ft (1,859m) Harts Pass (with the small town of Mazama 19 miles (30.4km) east down the road). Below in the valley are the remains of many mines that were once active here, producing gold, silver, copper, lead and zinc. Next the trail crosses the steep side of Slate Creek with good views to the west of the snow cone of Mount Baker. The drier nature of this region is noticeable with a lack of streams and sparse vegetation, plus a dusty veneer to the landscape. The red and yellow autumn colours were vivid, matching the brilliant strata of the rocks. In the next 8½ miles (13.6km) Buffalo, Windy, Foggy and Jim Passes are all crossed and the Pasayten Wilderness entered (at Windy Pass) and we arrive at a rocky spur called the Devil's Backbone. Here, the marvellous scenic walk ends temporarily as the trail zigzags steeply down to 5,050ft (1,515m) Holman Pass, thickly wooded with silver firs. However, a 1,200ft (360m) climb leads back up to a small campsite by a barely-flowing spring a mile or so

*The black bear, common throughout the mountains of North America, can cause problems as it can learn to raid campsites for food.*

Moonrise at dusk in the North Cascades.

Mica Lake.

before Rock Pass. Here I stopped for my last wilderness camp on the Pacific Crest Trail.

Dawn came with the sun struggling to pierce high, thin clouds. The peaks across the valley turned a dark sombre red before vanishing into the heavier clouds that quickly rolled in, bringing rain. My trek through the North Cascades looked like ending the way it had begun, with a storm. Again, as at the start of the walk, I saw little scenery as I scurried through the storm, head down against the increasing wind. From Rock Pass (6,491ft/1,947.3m) the trail drops into the Rock Creek valley, then climbs back up to the 6,624ft (1,987.2m) rock-filled and inaptly-named treeless Woody Pass. The next section, across open storm-blasted slopes, did give me a few views of rugged Three Fools Peak (7,930ft/2,379m). The grassy bench of Mountain Home Camp would be a good place to stop in better weather. I hurried on, driven by the storm, to climb to an unnamed 7,126ft (2,138m) summit on Lakeview Ridge with a view of pretty Hopkins Lake far below. The ridge is followed down to Hopkins Pass (6,122ft/1,836.5m). For once I welcomed my re-entry into the trees. This was not the weather for the high trails. Six and a half miles (10.4km) further along is Monument 78 on the United States–Canada border, a small bronze obelisk. Arriving here is an emotional moment if, as it did for me, it marks the completion of the 2,500 mile (4,000km) Pacific Crest Trail. I sat in the rain for a few minutes, trying to contemplate the long journey I'd undertaken, but the cold wet weather soon had me moving again for the last 7 forested miles (11.2km) to Highway 3. At the highway, buses can be caught and there is a lodge and a campground. The traverse of the North Cascades is over.

# THE ROUTE

| MILEAGE/(KM) | | PLACE | ELEVATION | |
|---|---|---|---|---|
| | | | ft | m |
| 0.0 | 0.0 | Snoqualmie Pass/Interstate 90 | 3,000 | 900 |
| 7.4 | 11.8 | Gravel Lake | 5,280 | 1,584 |
| 16.6 | 26.5 | Park Lakes Basin | 4,920 | 1,476 |
| 20.5 | 32.8 | Lemah Creek | 3,200 | 960 |
| 26.2 | 41.9 | Escondido Ridge high point | 5,520 | 1,656 |
| 35.7 | 57.1 | Waptus River | 3,040 | 912 |
| 43.2 | 69.1 | Deep Lake | 4,390 | 1,317 |
| 46.3 | 74.0 | Cathedral Pass | 5,610 | 1,683 |
| 51.5 | 82.4 | Deception Pass | 4,450 | 1,335 |
| 54.6 | 87.3 | Deception Lakes | 5,053 | 1,515.9 |
| 56.4 | 90.2 | Glacier Lake | 5,000 | 1,500 |
| 58.7 | 93.9 | Trap Pass | 5,800 | 1,740 |
| 69.9 | 111.8 | Stevens Pass/Highway 2 | 4,060 | 1,218 |
| 75.5 | 120.8 | Lake Valhalla | 4,830 | 1,449 |
| 79.5 | 127.2 | Janice Cabin | 4,150 | 1,245 |
| 88.2 | 141.1 | Pear Lake | 4,809 | 1,442.7 |
| 98.1 | 156.9 | Lake Sally Ann | 5,479 | 1,643.7 |
| 108.6 | 173.7 | Red Pass | 6,500 | 1,950 |
| 119.4 | 191.0 | Glacier Creek | 5,640 | 1,692 |
| 124.7 | 199.5 | Fire Creek Pass | 6,350 | 1,905 |
| 128.7 | 205.9 | Milk Creek | 3,800 | 1,050 |
| 134.0 | 214.4 | Dolly Vista campsite | 5,830 | 1,749 |
| 141.5 | 226.4 | Suiattle River | 2,860 | 858 |
| 150.9 | 241.4 | Suiattle Pass | 5,983 | 1,794.9 |
| 155.5 | 248.8 | Hemlock Camp | 3,560 | 1,068 |
| 162.5 | 260.0 | Five Mile Camp | 2,160 | 648 |
| 167.5 | 268.0 | Agnes Creek/Stehekin River road | 1,650 | 495 |
| 186.6 | 298.5 | Rainy Pass/Highway 20 | 4,855 | 1,456.5 |
| 191.7 | 306.7 | Cutthroat Pass | 6,820 | 2,046 |
| 197.2 | 315.5 | Methow Pass | 6,600 | 1,980 |
| 207.8 | 332.4 | Glacier Pass | 5,520 | 1,656 |
| 222.3 | 355.6 | Windy Pass | 6,257 | 1,877.1 |
| 230.9 | 369.4 | Holman Pass | 5,050 | 1,515 |
| 236.8 | 378.8 | Woody Pass | 6,624 | 1,987.2 |
| 248.5 | 397.6 | Monument 78 – US/Canada border | 4,240 | 1,272 |
| 255.7 | 409.1 | Manning Park/Highway 3 | 3,800 | 1,140 |

The trailhead is on **Interstate 90** at **Snoqualmie Pass** (3,000ft, Mile 0). Signed the Pacific Crest Trail, the route starts to climb after just ¼ mile, switchbacking up into the Alpine Lakes Wilderness before traversing across scree slopes on a narrow path and then ledges blasted out of the rock to a pass between Ridge and **Gravel Lakes** (5,280ft, Mile 7.4). Four more miles of exposed trail on and below a narrow crest lead to tiny Needle Site Gap where a long traverse of Chickamin Ridge is begun, ending with a descent into the **Park Lakes Basin** (4,920ft, Mile 16.6). After crossing one more saddle, the switchbacking descent continues down to a bridged crossing of **Lemah Creek** (3,200ft, Mile 20.5) from where the next ascent leads up to a cirque near the top of **Escondido Ridge** (5,520ft, Mile 26.2). A lengthy descent then switchbacks down to the **Waptus River** (3,040ft, Mile 35.7), from where a gentle climb leads gradually up above hidden Waptus Lake to enter the Spinola Creek basin which the trail traverses high above the creek, before switchbacking up the western wall and then descending to cross the creek and reach **Deep Lake** (4,390ft, Mile 43.2). Steeply climbing, the trail heads up to **Cathedral Pass** (5,610ft, Mile 46.3) to descend back to 3,800ft in the next 3½ miles and then reascend a little to **Deception Pass** (4,450ft, Mile 51.5). A wooded traverse leads to **Deception Lakes** from where the old Cascade Crest Trail can be taken to Surprise Gap, rejoining the PCT after 1½ miles. The PCT route via Pieper Pass is twice as long. **Glacier Lake** is ¼ mile past the junction of the two alternative routes (5,000ft, Mile 56.4). The trail continues northwards over **Trap Pass** (5,800ft, Mile 58.7) to a long, high level crest that is left for a descent to ski tows, powerlines, **Highway 2** and **Stevens Pass** (4,060ft, Mile 69.9). From the road, the trail is in forest before switchbacking up to a saddle and then descending to **Lake Valhalla** (4,830ft, Mile 75.5). Running ever northwards the trail continues its rollercoaster progress to Janus Lake and spacious **Janice Cabin** (4,150ft, Mile 79.5), then follows the crest of the mountains again over the shoulder of Grizzly Peak and down to Wenatchee Pass and then, in 1½ miles more, **Pear Lake** (4,809ft, Mile 88.2). From the lake, up we go again to Frozen Finger Gap (5,250ft) down to Fortune Pond (4,670ft), up to a ridge (5,220ft) and down and up again to Saddle Gap (5,060ft) before a longer ascent leads past **Lake Sally Ann** (5,479ft, Mile 98.1) to Wards Pass (5,710ft) and another ridge route to Indian Pass (5,020ft) and then up higher than before to **Red Pass** (6,500ft, Mile 108.6). A long descent leads down into the White Chuck River valley to a low point at **Chetwot Creek** (3,730ft, Mile 116.1). Now in the Glacier Peak Wilderness, we climb to **Glacier Creek** and then **Fire Creek Pass** (6,350ft, Mile 124.7) and then drop down past Mica Lake to **Milk Creek** (3,800ft, Mile 128.7). The next ridge is reached

after a 2½ mile, 2,000ft climb, a high point of 6,010ft being reached before the next descent commences past the **Dolly Vista campsite** (5,830ft, Mile 134) all the way down to the **Suiattle River** (2,860ft, Mile 141.5). A final ascent in the Glacier Peak Wilderness leads up to **Suiattle Pass** (5,983ft, Mile 150.9), before the long descent of the South Fork **Agnes Creek** is undertaken all the way to the **Stehekin River road** (1,650ft, Mile 167.5). In another ¾ mile we enter the North Cascades National Park and begin the long ascent beside Bridge Creek to **Highway 20** and **Rainy Pass** (4,855ft, Mile 186.6). Across the highway, the climb continues in the Porcupine Creek drainage up to **Cutthroat Pass** (6,820ft, Mile 191.7) and a narrow cresthugging route to Granite Pass (6,290ft) and then on through easier, though still open terrain to **Methow Pass** (6,600ft, Mile 197.2) and a descent into the basin of the **West Fork Methow River** which is crossed on a bridge (4,370ft, Mile 202.1). Back up again, the trail swoops and dives over a series of passes (**Glacier**, Harts, Buffalo, **Windy**, Foggy, Jim, **Holman**, Rock, **Woody**, Hopkins and Castle are the named ones) in the next 40 miles. Through this section, we cross the Harts Pass Road (No 374) before entering the Pasayten Wilderness just beyond Windy Pass (6,257ft, Mile 222.3) and then traversing round Jim Peak and over the rocky spur of the Devil's Backbone. Beyond Woody Pass (6,624ft, Mile 236.8) the slopes of Three Fools Peak are traversed to an unnamed summit on Lakeview Ridge (7,126ft) before, after crossing 5,451ft Castle Pass, the trail descends to the **United States/Canada border** and **Monument 78** (4,240ft, Mile 248.5). A final viewless 7 miles leads through **Manning Park** to **Highway 3** (3,800ft, Mile 255.7).

# GUIDEBOOK AND MAPS

*The Pacific Crest Trail Vol. 2: Oregon and Washington* by Jeffrey P. Schaffer and A. Selters has 1:50,000 topographic maps for the whole trail. Supplement with the *Pacific Crest Trail Pocket Guide*.

# The Great Divide Trail:
## Mount Shark to Cataract Brook   105 miles (168km)

*People who know the value of something are inclined to cherish and protect it. The Canadian Rockies – beautiful, savage, delicate, unique – are worthy indeed.*

Ben Gadd   *The Handbook of the Canadian Rockies*

The Rocky Mountains stretch northwards from the border with the USA for 850 miles (1,360km) through Canada to terminate in northern British Columbia. There is far more untouched wilderness in these mountains than anywhere else in North America outside of the Yukon and Alaska. The southern half of the Canadian Rockies are the best known, with much of the area protected in national and provincial parks and wilderness areas; the mountain park belt. Here, the watershed of North America, known in Canada as the Great Divide, threads its way along the crest of the highest peaks, the Main Ranges. Plans have been made to create a Great Divide Trail from the border with the USA all the way to Mount Robson, the highest summit in the range, but no such trail yet exists and it may never do so. Trails can be linked in some areas, however, to make such a route and suggestions for a route in the mountain parks are outlined in Patton and Robinson's *Canadian Rockies Trail Guide*. It is the part of this route that follows most closely the Divide itself that is described here.

The Canadian Rockies are alpine in nature and heavily glaciated, but the sedimentary rock from which they are carved gives them a distinctive appearance, unique to the range. This is a northern wilderness with dense conifer forests and wildlife, including grizzly and black bears, grey wolf, wolverine, lynx, moose, elk and beaver. In summer, the meadows are rich with wildflowers, but the season only lasts about six weeks with autumn starting in late August, earlier above timberline. Although short, the summer is warm and reasonably dry, July being the best month.

The walk passes through three national parks, Banff, Kootenay and Yoho, plus Mount Assiniboine Provincial Park and is all on good, signposted trails. Although there are many steep climbs and the route passes through rugged mountain terrain, these trails plus the provision of backcountry campgrounds with bear poles for hanging food from at regular intervals, bridged creeks and rivers and plenty of escape routes, make this a walk that should be well within the capabilities of any competent backpacker. Well-maintained trails with signposts at all junctions make route-finding easy. I never used my compass and found my maps most useful for identifying distant peaks and gaining an overall view of the area, rather than for navigation.

There are no supply points on the route, although meals can be purchased at the ski resort of Sunshine Village 35 miles (56km) into the route and afternoon tea at Lake O'Hara

Mount Assiniboine and Lake Magog.

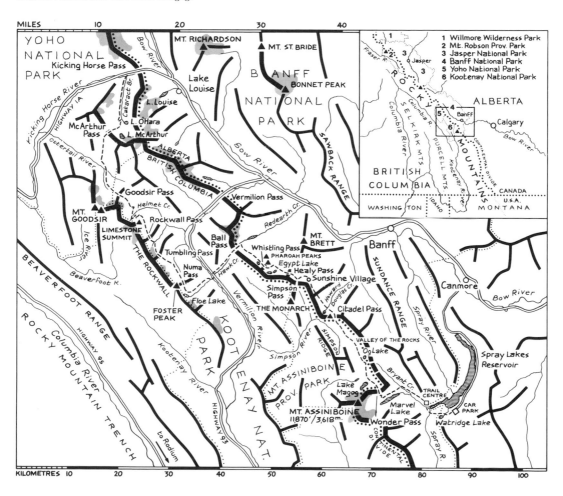

Lodge after 97 miles (155.2km). From Sunshine Village the gondola can be taken down to a road where buses can be caught to the town of Lake Louise. Sunshine Village will also hold food parcels for you if you take them up there as I did once on a spring ski tour. Backcountry permits are needed for the national parks. They can be obtained for the whole walk at the National Park Visitor Centre in Banff townsite before you start, along with any recent bear warnings and trail alterations. If you intend using the very popular campground at Lake O'Hara, this should be booked in advance with the date when you'll be there, as it's full most nights during the summer. There is a charge for staying at the Naiset Cabins and the Lake Magog Campground in Mount Assiniboine Provincial Park, so take some cash with you if you intend to use either of these. There are many possible side trips and excursions along the route but as described it shouldn't take much more than a week.

The Mount Shark Trailhead where the route begins, lies at the end of the large Spray Lakes Reservoir 24 miles (38.4km) from the town of Canmore. From the parking lot a wide trail leads for nearly 4 miles (6.4km) past Watridge Lake to the rather grandly named Trail Centre where there is a noticeboard and trail sign. When I was last here, this first section was a muddy quagmire, but there was much trail work going on, so by now it's hopefully a good path. From the Trail Centre the route takes the Bryant Creek Trail, passing the Bryant Creek Shelter after 4 miles (6.4km). This is open to walkers, but quite likely to be well populated. Half a mile further on is the Bryant Creek Warden Cabin and a campground plus a trail junction. If the weather is bad I would suggest staying on the Bryant Creek Trail from here and crossing 7,100ft (2,130m) Assiniboine Pass as this is the easiest, shortest and most sheltered way into Lake Magog and Mount Assiniboine.

However, a much more scenic, if more strenuous route is that by Marvel Lake and Wonder Pass. From the junction, the route contours high above the dark forest-shrouded lake before climbing steeply for 1,250ft (375m) to 7,850ft (2,355m) Wonder Pass. Throughout, there are superb views of the peaks and glaciers at the head of the lake and then from the pass a fantastic view north all the way to the mountains around Sunshine Meadows where we are headed. A gentle descent leads down past Gog Lake to Lake Magog at the foot of Mount Assiniboine. There are cabins in the woods by the lake, which are rented out by the Forest Service (there is a warden here) on a firstcome, first-served basis, and private accommodation, bookable in advance, at Assiniboine Lodge. Across the lake is a campground.

Mount Assiniboine Provincial Park is 240.6 miles$^2$ (385km$^2$) in size and surrounds the mountain it is named after, an 11,870ft (3,561m) towering snow and rock pyramid known as 'the Matterhorn of the Rockies' and in my view, one of the most impressive individual peaks in the range. It was on seeing pictures of this peak that I was first drawn to the Canadian Rockies and I have visited it twice, once in spring on skis from Sunshine Village, and once in summer on the route detailed here. The park is a wilderness one, not reachable by road, although there are regular helicopter flights from Canmore that land near the lodge, flights I'd been grateful for on the ski tour as rotten spring snow made skiing out via Assiniboine Pass almost impossible.

On that visit I'd stayed with two others in one of the Naiset Cabins, the warmth of a wood-burning stove much to be preferred to the damp confines of the tent. During our first night here we'd been woken during the night by a shatteringly loud, abrasive sound reminiscent of a chainsaw outside the cabin. 'Porcupine,' muttered Jari and rushed outside with a broom. The noise stopped. Within minutes it began again. 'Someone else's turn,' said Jari. Reluctantly, I plodded out half-naked into the freezing night. The snow on the sloping roof of the cabin reached down to the ground, leaving a narrow tunnel between it and the walls. In this tunnel, a large porcupine was busy trying to eat the cabin. I tried to poke it with the broom, but couldn't reach it. I was loath to crawl into the tunnel. Those spines looked large. Instead I climbed, barefoot, on to the roof of the cabin and tried to poke the broom through the snow from above. I was partially successful, but twice fell and slid off the roof in a cloud of snow and curses. The porcupine remained where it was. Finally, I lay down in the mouth of the tunnel and lobbed snowballs at the beast. It didn't like this and edged towards the far end. I slung a few more snowballs. The porcupine made a dash for the nearest trees. Wanting to discourage it from even thinking of coming back I pursued it, yelling loudly and waving the broom while staggering wildly across the knee-deep snow. The animal climbed a tree very quickly and, cold, scratched, bruised and exhausted, I returned to the cabin to find the other two convulsed with laughter. 'That sounded hilarious,' they said. I crept back into the warm depths of my sleeping bag.

Now that was an extreme occurrence, but porcupines and other animals can be a nuisance, as I was reminded at the Lake Magog campground on my second visit by the ground squirrels that tried to steal my trail mix. As well as hanging your food to keep it safe from bears in the Canadian Rockies, I would suggest keeping everything else, especially your boots which porcupines will gnaw for the salt from your sweaty feet, in the tent.

From Lake Magog to Citadel Pass on the boundary with Banff National Park is a distance of 12 miles (19.2km). I set out on this route after a beautiful clear dawn, turning back time after time to look back across the lake to

*Trail sign, Mount Assiniboine Provincial Park.*

glacier-clad Mount Assiniboine, from the top of which trailed a white, wind-blown plume of cloud. The trail leads past Og Lake where there is a campground and into the unusual Valley of the Rocks, where it takes a complex route through boulder-strewn forest. I met many people on this section as most walkers heading for Assiniboine come in via the Sunshine Village ski lift, as there is then very little ascent involved. Heading north the backpacker is faced with a long and steep climb up to Citadel Pass, at 7,740ft (2,322m), an ascent eased for me by the wonderful display of wild flowers on the open slopes below the pass and kept cool by several showers of rain.

Once over Citadel Pass, the walker enters the vast undulating subalpine flower-filled Sunshine Meadows through which runs the Great Divide. This is vulnerable much-visited terrain, so it's important to stay on the trail, which, as the ski resort draws near, becomes a gravel walkway carefully edged and graded.

Mount Assiniboine.

Citadel Peak and Mount Assiniboine seen over the Sunshine Meadows.

Before this developed trail is reached, Howard Douglas Lake and campground are passed. My walk here from Lake Magog took eight hours, rather a change from my ski tour over a year earlier when it had taken two of us four days to do the same journey in the other and easier direction. On that occasion bad weather, a broken ski binding and soft snow had conspired to double the time we thought the trek would take.

The view south from the higher points on this trail are excellent, with Mount Assiniboine, 10 aerial miles away now, towering over the surrounding tops. The intrusion of the ski resort of Sunshine Village is soon passed (although the inn is a nice place for some 'real' food, or as a shelter from bad weather) and a section of high passes and deep valleys is traversed, the closed-in terrain a total contrast to the open landscape of Sunshine Meadows.

Wawa Ridge, immediately above the resort, is crossed first and gives good views of the meadows, the last we'll have, and Mount Assiniboine from its crest. After descending to unmemorable Simpson Pass, named for Sir George Simpson of the Hudson's Bay Company who crossed it while searching for a new route for fur traders across the Rockies in 1841, the trail climbs and then runs beneath the rock spur of Monarch Ramparts before ascending Healy Pass, at 7,650ft (2,295m), which gives good views all around including, almost inevitably, the distant Mount Assiniboine, although this is the last clear view you'll have of that peak. West of the pass can be seen the clustered Pharaoh Peaks where we are headed.

A descent leads to the highly popular yet, in my view, not very attractive forest-shaded Egypt Lake Campground, where there is a shelter. I'd intended to camp here, but there

were so many people about with tents pitched everywhere that, even though it was evening, I went on to climb steeply up to the rocky 7,550ft (2,265m) pass called Whistling Valley (named I discovered not for the wind that whips through it, but for the hoary marmots that whistle in warning from the rocks when backpackers pass by) and views of the Ball Range. Three and a half miles and 1,250ft (375m) of descent from the pass is Ball Pass Junction Campground, a beautiful, quiet, scenic timberline site featuring some picnic tables, so called because it lies at the intersection of two major trails. I had the place to myself, apart from a couple of porcupines that tried to run off with my pack.

Banff National Park is finally left for Kootenay National Park at Ball Pass which lies 1½ miles (2.4km) and 1,000ft (300m) above the campground. The view from the pass is dominated by Mount Ball, a distinctive, bulky peak capped with a curving white glacier. I sat here awhile absorbing the view, not relishing the long descent to come. Some people dread ascents, personally I dislike descents more for the jarring they give the knees and back. The one down from Ball Pass is a real pounder as it takes the walker down 2,900ft (870m) in 6 miles (9.6km) on a rocky, dry trail. Near its foot, there is a campground just beyond which the Banff – Radium Highway is crossed and a 2,350ft (705m) climb commenced through dense, cooling forest to Floe Lake, an ascent that took me three hours.

Floe Lake is an unbelievably beautiful timberline lake stretched out between the forest and the 3,000ft (900m) sheer cliffs of the massive Rockwall. Beneath the cliffs lie small glaciers that in summer carve off small ice floes, hence the lake's name. A campground lies on the forested shore, a large site with many facilities, including gravel tent pads as the lake is a popular destination. From its shores starts the Rockwall Trail, one of the finest mountain trails I have ever walked, which runs along the base of the 25 mile (40km) long limestone wall, with the Great Divide running along its crest, for nearly 20 miles (32km). The trail is not level as it soars and dips over three high passes and down into forested canyons, past waterfalls, flower-filled cirques, hanging glaciers and magnificent alpine scenery.

*Female elk in Banff National Park.*

Dawn at Floe Lake was impressive, as the slowly increasing light gradually lit the distant snows far to the south and then crept under a pink sky along the length of the lake to turn the grey cliffs and dull dirty snow a warm gold and brilliant white. I was to be blessed by hot, clear weather for the whole of my walk beneath the Rockwall. The trail begins by ascending to Numa Pass under the pyramid of Foster Peak, at 7,725ft (2,317.5m) the highest point on this section of the route, and then switchbacking steeply downwards to 5,000ft (1,500m) Numa Creek and a campground. Immediately the trail heads back up via an open avalanche slope to Tumbling Pass, (7,250ft/2,175m) where there are excellent views back to Foster Peak, a summit that dominates views south along the Rockwall throughout the walk. Descending again, the trail drops to 6,200ft (1,860m) at Tumbling Creek where there is a campground. Here I stopped to pitch the tent on the edge of a meadow and sat watching the evening light highlighting the curving arêtes and jagged blocks of snow high up on the Tumbling Glacier. Later in the evening, a thin crescent moon rose above the darkening mountain wall.

Again my only companions in camp were porcupines, which this time tried to steal my boots, waking me in the process. Although they were smelling of stale sweat, I brought the boots into the tent. Bright dawn light on the cliffs promised another fine day as I shivered in the sunless meadow over breakfast. The steep 1,250ft (375m) climb up to Wolverine Plateau soon warmed me up. For the next 3½ miles (5.6km) the trail stays high with no descents as it crosses Rockwall Pass and Limestone Summit. The views along the Rockwall in either direction are superb and I thought this the finest section of a fine trail. An extra bonus was the sight of a herd of mountain goats browsing on a low crag. From Limestone Summit, at 7,115ft (2,134.5m) the trail drops 1,400ft (420m) in 2 miles (3.2km) to the Helmet

Creek valley where Helmet Falls tumbles 1,200ft (360m) down the vast amphitheatre that marks the northern end of the Rockwall. As I descended through the forest I heard the thunder of the falls long before it suddenly came into view across an avalanche chute, surprizingly far away for the volume of noise.

The Rockwall left behind now, the trail climbs again for 1,500ft (450m) and 2½ miles (4km) to the wide, flower-filled alpine meadows of Goodsir Pass, where a park warden on horseback told me there were signs of recent grizzly bear activity. Ahead tower the twin peaks of Mount Goodsir, at 11,700ft (3,510m) the highest in Yoho National Park which is entered at the pass, while behind stretches out the Rockwall all the way south to the still distinct pyramid of Foster Peak. The descent from the pass to the Ottertail River is long (2,400ft/720m) and waterless, and in thick forest that seems airless on a hot day. I carried no water and regretted it, arriving at the river dry and dusty. At the river, the route turns downstream past the McArthur Creek Warden Cabin to the McArthur Campground situated in dense lodgepole pine forest, where I camped, although I set up my kitchen on the banks of the Ottertail, marvelling at the view of the northeast face of Mount Goodsir rising 6,200ft (1,860m) from Goodsir Creek, a phenomenal mountain wall.

The 2,400ft (720m) climb to the last pass on the route, McArthur Pass (7,250ft/2,175m) is arduous but there are many opportunities to stop and look back over the thickly vegetated avalanche chutes it traverses to the soaring peaks of Mount Goodsir. The rich plant and animal life of the McArthur Creek valley attracts grizzlies and I saw much fresh dung on the trail as I ascended. A warden I met near the top of the pass said three bears were active in the area. The *Trail Guide* warns of grizzlies here too, so it would be advisable to be extra cautious when in this valley. The warden also

*Floe Lake campground.*

*Floe Lake and the Rockwall.*

*Early morning sun on the Rockwall seen from the Tumbling Creek Campground.*

advised me against the Duchesnay Pass route out to the highway from Lake O'Hara as described in the guidebook (which does say it is for experienced backpackers only), saying that the trailless route involved some dangerous scrambling and also that it crossed some important fossil beds on a trail closed to the general public.

From McArthur Pass it is a short walk to Lake O'Hara, situated in spectacular alpine scenery and boasting a shuttle bus from the highway below, an impressive private lodge where afternoon tea can be had if you arrive in time to place a reservation (if not, there are soft drinks and candy bars for sale), Alpine Club of Canada cabins, a warden cabin, and a busy campground. The variety of walks and climbs radiating from the area make it a popular

base for day trips. An extensive trail system visits just about every lake, cirque and ridge in the area.

To reach the road in the valley below, you could walk down the Lake O'Hara access road (closed to public traffic), but far better is to descend the trail on the west side of the Cataract Brook valley. This route, mostly in forest, provides several good views of the peaks around the lake and above the creek, as well as those across the highway to the north. It's 8 miles (12.8km) down the trail to the roadhead and the end of the Great Divide walk. A café lies on the Trans-Canada Highway a short distance away and from the highway, buses can be caught to Lake Louise and Banff. For those who wish to walk further, north of the highway lies the Yoho Valley and some fine trails, although there is no easy through-route and if you don't want to undertake difficult cross-country travel and risky stream fords you will have to return to the road. For those who do wish to continue north, I suggest a route along the Iceline Trail to Little Yoho Valley and then over Kiwetinok and Amiskwi Passes to the Blaeberry River and a return to Banff National Park at Howse Pass, but be prepared for some rough country.

## THE ROUTE

| MILEAGE/(KM) | | PLACE | ELEVATION | |
|---|---|---|---|---|
| | | | ft | m |
| 0.0 | 0.0 | Watridge Creek | 5,600 | 1,680 |
| 3.7 | 5.9 | Trail Centre | 5,600 | 1,680 |
| 8.5 | 13.6 | Bryant Creek Warden Cabin | 6,050 | 1,815 |
| 14.0 | 22.4 | Wonder Pass | 7,850 | 2,355 |
| 16.8 | 26.8 | Lake Magog Campground | 7,100 | 2,130 |
| 21.0 | 33.6 | Og Lake | 6,755 | 2,026.5 |
| 29.0 | 46.4 | Citadel Pass | 7,740 | 2,322 |
| 34.8 | 55.6 | Sunshine Village | 7,200 | 2,160 |
| 40.5 | 64.8 | Healy Pass | 7,650 | 2,295 |
| 42.5 | 68.0 | Egypt Lake Campground | 6,545 | 1,963.5 |
| 44.6 | 71.3 | Whistling Pass | 7,545 | 2,263.5 |
| 48.0 | 76.8 | Ball Pass Junction Campground | 6,300 | 1,890 |
| 49.7 | 79.5 | Ball Pass | 7,250 | 2,175 |
| 55.7 | 89.1 | Banff–Radium Highway | 4,345 | 1,303.5 |
| 62.2 | 99.5 | Floe Lake | 6,700 | 2.010 |
| 63.8 | 102.0 | Numa Pass | 7,725 | 2,317.5 |
| 71.3 | 114.0 | Tumbling Pass | 7,250 | 2,175 |
| 75.1 | 120.1 | Rockwall Pass | 7,350 | 2,205 |
| 78.2 | 125.1 | Limestone Summit | 7,115 | 2,134.5 |
| 80.5 | 128.8 | Rockwall Trail/Helmet Creek Trail junction | 5,770 | 1,731 |
| 83.0 | 132.8 | Goodsir Pass | 7,250 | 2,175 |
| 88.2 | 141.1 | Ottertail River | 4,855 | 1,456.5 |
| 95.7 | 153.1 | McArthur Pass | 7,250 | 2,175 |
| 97.0 | 155.2 | Lake O'Hara | 6,675 | 2,002.5 |
| 105.0 | 168 | Trailhead/1-A Highway | 5,250 | 1,575 |

The trailhead is the Mount Shark parking lot above **Watridge Creek** (5,600ft, Mile 0) where the road from the town of Canmore along the southern side of the Spray Lakes Reservoir ends. A wide, recently maintained trail leads past Watridge Lake to the **Trail Centre** trailhead at the head of the reservoir, where there is a large map and noticeboard. An alternative is to drive to Canyon Dam on the north shore of the reservoir and walk to Trail Centre along the old road (passable by four-wheel drive vehicles), which adds ½ mile to the route. From the Trail Centre, enter Banff National Park and take the trail sign-posted for Bryant Creek (5,600ft, Mile 3.7) to **Bryant Creek Warden Cabin** (6,050ft, Mile 8.5), where it is left for the trail to Marvel

Lake and **Wonder Pass** which contours above the lake and then switchbacks up to Wonder Pass (7,850ft, Mile 14), to enter Mount Assiniboine Provincial Park and descend slightly to **Lake Magog** (7,100ft, Mile 16.8). From the lake, follow the trail to **Citadel Pass** (7,740ft, Mile 29), past **Og Lake** and through the Valley of the Rocks to re-enter Banff National Park and descend past Howard Douglas Lake and through the Sunshine Meadows to the ski resort of **Sunshine Village** (7,200ft, Mile 34.8). The trail then leads over Simpson and **Healy Passes** to the popular **Egypt Lake Campground** (6,545ft, Mile 42.5) and then up to **Whistling Pass** and down to the **Ball Pass Junction Campground** (6,300ft, Mile 48). A climb leads to **Ball Pass** (7,250ft, Mile 49.7), entry into Kootenay National Park and a long descent in the Hawk Creek valley to the **Banff–Radium Highway** (4,345ft, Mile 55.7). Across the highway, the trail climbs straight back up to **Floe Lake** (6,700ft, Mile 62.2) and the start of the Rockwall Trail which is followed over **Numa**, **Tumbling** and **Rockwall Passes** to **Limestone Summit** (7,115ft, Mile 78.2) and a descent to the trails end at a junction with the **Helmet Creek Trail** (5,770ft, Mile 80.5), which is taken back up to **Goodsir Pass** (7,250ft, Mile 83) and entry into Yoho National Park. A long descent leads down to the **Ottertail River** (4,855ft, Mile 88.2) to be followed by an equally long ascent to **McArthur Pass** (7,250ft, Mile 95.7) just over which the trail arrives at **Lake O'Hara** (6,675ft, Mile 97). From the lake a final descent leads down the Cataract Brook valley to a parking lot by the **1-A Highway** (5,250ft, Mile 105).

## MAPS

1:50,000 topographic maps: Spray Lakes Reservoir; Mount Assiniboine; Banff; Mount Goodsir; Lake Louise. National Park 1:200,000: Banff–Yoho–Kootenay map.

## RECOMMENDED GUIDEBOOK

*The Canadian Rockies Trail Guide* by Brian Patton and Bart Robinson (Summerthought).

# The Glacier and Skyline Trails: Norman Creek to Maligne Lake Road 105 miles (168km)

*Every time I go anywhere out in the desert or mountains I wonder why I should return. Someday, I won't.*

Edward Abbey  *Abbey's Road*

East of the Main Ranges of the Canadian Rockies lie the Front Ranges, so called, because, just like Colorado's Front Range over 1,500 miles (2,400km) to the south (*see* Chapter 2), they are the first peaks encountered as you travel west across the great plains, a vast mountain wall rising up to block the view. Although not quite as high as the Main Ranges (the highest peak is Mount Brazeau at 11,380ft (3,414m) near Maligne Lake) and with fewer glaciers, the Front Ranges are rugged alpine peaks with a distinctive character of their own

*Backpacker on the Glacier Trail by the Brazeau River bridge.*

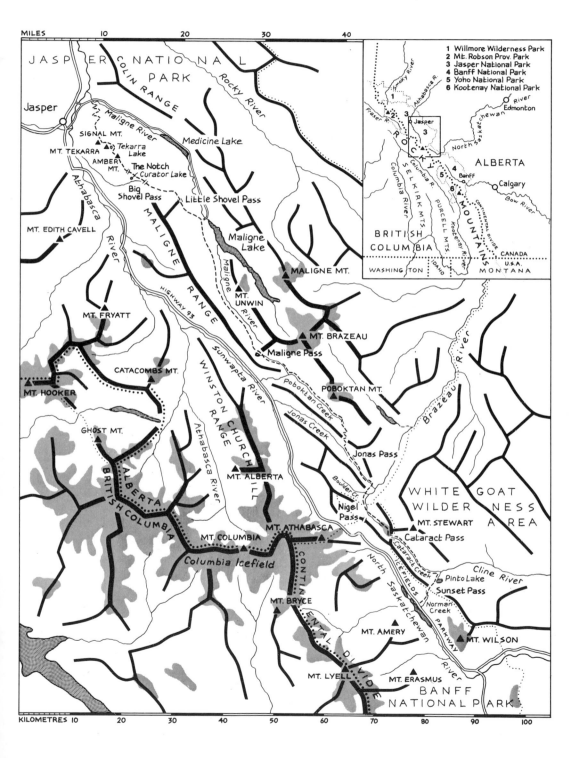

and it is through them that this route wanders, mostly in Jasper National Park, although with a start in Banff National Park and a brief excursion into the White Goat Wilderness Area.

The first section of the route, the Glacier Trail, is all that is left of a trip pioneered by outfitter Jack Brewster in 1924, because the sections at either end now feature metalled roads. But the highest and wildest 76 miles (121.6km) is left for the backpacker to explore, a superb walk through long valleys and over high passes. At Maligne Lake where there is a roadhead and a café (but no grocery store), the second part of the route starts. This is the Skyline Trail, an aptly-named mountain pathway that leads up to traverse the crest of the Front Ranges before descending to the Maligne Lake Road. The Skyline Trail is 27 miles (43.2km) long, over half of which is above timberline.

For most of the route there are good trails, but those for the 20 miles (32km) in the White Goat Wilderness are sketchy and unsigned with no bridges over the creeks. For those who wish to avoid this part of the route, there is an alternate start via Nigel Pass which shortens the route by about 20 miles (32km). There are no supply points *en route* (although you can buy, as I did, 'rolls, cake slices and little cartons of butter and cheese' at the Maligne Lake café if necessary), but the whole route should take no more than ten days and can easily be done in a week. If the weather turns bad or you run out of time or food, you can escape down the road from Maligne Lake to Jasper townsite. Permits are needed for the national park sections and can be obtained in the National Park Visitor Centres in either Banff or Jasper townsites.

The walk starts unpromisingly with a steep climb in dense forest from the trailhead on the Icefields Parkway. A brief glimpse of the Norman Creek gorge is the only view as the trail switchbacks up waterless slopes. If it's hot, a full water bottle would be welcome on this stretch. I was lucky in that there was a cooling westerly breeze as I climbed slowly up behind a six horse-one man pack train meeting *en route* a couple of hikers descending at speed who stopped to say how good the scenery was once the climb was over. They were right, as I found when I emerged into the vast meadows that stretch for over 2 miles (3.2km) to Sunset Pass. To the north rises Mount Coleman, its horizontal strata prominent, while to the west, over the North Saskatchewan Valley, the Main Range summits of Mounts Amery and Saskatchewan dominate the view. On the southern edge of the meadows is the Norman Creek Campground where I camped, alone except for an ermine that sped through the site, zipping in and out of squirrel holes. Late in the evening, I was woken by a party of anglers arriving, shining torches and talking loudly as they crossed the meadows in the dark in case there were any bears around. By the time I woke in the morning they had gone.

From 7,100ft (2,130m) Sunset Pass on the eastern edge of the meadows, the trail drops abruptly out of Banff National Park, into the White Goat Wilderness Area and down to large Pinto Lake, where there are good campsites and whose shore the trail brushes. In Canadian Rockies wilderness areas, unlike in the USA, there is no trail maintenance and I found lots of fallen trees along the otherwise clearly defined trail that leads to fords of Huntington and Cataract Creeks. Again, there are no bridges in wilderness areas. I kept my feet dry by crossing on large log jams I found upstream of the trail fords, but, of course, these may not be present every year. A long ascent beside Cataract Creek on a rough trail, although quite a clear one until timberline is reached, leads to a large alpine bowl replete with flower meadows and ringed by hanging glaciers, rock peaks and golden scree slopes where several people were camping when I passed through. I was tempted to join them, as camping is allowed anywhere in wilderness areas, but soon abandoned this idea when I saw fresh grizzly bear diggings in the meadows. These large piles of fresh earth are made by bears digging for ground squirrels and marmots. As there was nowhere to hang my food, I didn't want to risk camping in an area where bears were active.

Cataract Pass (8,250ft/2,475m), to the west of the bowl is quite obvious and the climb to it steep, but on generally good firm terrain although there are a few patches of scree and the odd snowpatch to be crossed. The descent into the valley of the south fork of the Brazeau River is not on grassy slopes and stable stones, but on steep loose scree and talus. There is a path slanting across the slopes to the north, but the start isn't clear from above and I missed it and ended up slithering straight down the unstable debris to a grey moraine lake at the foot of a small glacier. Keep right from the pass and you should pick the path up. No trail leads down the valley below, but the way is obvious and the alpine valley, although austere, is quite beautiful, especially in late evening light.

Three and three-quarter miles (6km) from Cataract Pass, the alternative route over Nigel Pass is met. To reach this point directly, start from a trailhead on the Icefields Parkway and climb steeply to 7,200ft (2,160m) Nigel Pass and then descend a short way to a ford of the south fork of the Brazeau River. The distance is just 5 miles (8km). The trail from Nigel Pass leads down the valley to a bridge over the Brazeau River and the small Boulder Creek Campground where I camped. Unlike the backcountry sites in the other Canadian national parks, those in Jasper do not have bear poles with cables and pulleys, just wooden poles nailed between two trees so you will have to provide your own line for hanging your food. One hiker who was just setting up his tent as I

arrived had forgotten his and was planning on leaving his food on the ground until I offered him use of my cord, as much for my own peace of mind as to protect his food. As well as his food, it turned out he'd forgotten both his boots (he was wearing black city shoes!) and his map, but I couldn't help him with those. He was also, unsurprisingly, lost and should have been the other side of Cataract Pass, where he headed the next day.

The route continues down the valley to a junction with the Jonas Pass Trail just beyond the Four Point Campground. Leaving the Brazeau River here, the route climbs through an open forest to a long (8 mile (12.8km)) above-timberline section over Jonas Pass to a high point of 8,100ft (2,430m) on Jonas Shoulder. As I headed up this trail the skies darkened and once out of the trees I found myself in a grey, desolate landscape with a cold wind blowing across it. Hurrying up beside the noisy creek I wasn't paying much attention to what was around me, when I caught a glimpse of something moving away to my right on the far bank. I looked more closely, then stopped with shock. A hundred yards (90m) away was a massive grizzly bear coming towards me. Its nose was to the ground and once my initial panic was over I realized it probably wasn't aware I was there, grizzlies having poor eyesight, but a good sense of smell and good hearing. The last two senses would have been hindered by the creek and the wind. To alert the bear to my presence I waved my arms, shouted loudly (very loudly!) and blew my orange plastic safety whistle. The performance seemed to work as the bear, after pausing momentarily, headed away from me down the creek bank. I moved away in the other direction until I felt at a safe distance, then stopped and sat on the hillside watching the bear through my binoculars as it slowly meandered down the hillside, turning over boulders and snuffling through the bushes in search of food.

*The grizzly bear, found throughout the Canadian Rockies, provides for a scary encounter when met at close quarters.*

This encounter, a fairly typical one, with this magnificent symbol of the wilderness was a highlight of the walk.

The grizzly having gone into the willow scrub, I continued up the bleak valley to the long heart of the pass past a small pond before descending a little and then climbing steeply on a slanting traverse up the ridge of Jonas Shoulder to the north. The views from the shoulder were extensive, if hazy. In clear conditions this must be a superlative viewpoint. Below can be seen the long, darkly-forested Poboktan Creek valley, down which the route runs. Two miles down from the ridge and just below timberline, we reach a junction with the Poboktan Creek Trail and the Jonas Cutoff Campground. Here I stopped to set up camp and chat to several other backpackers who were there, including another solo hiker who'd met the same bear as me, but on the trail at a distance of only about 50ft (15m), and also a female grizzly with two cubs.

*(Preceding pages) Sunset Pass Meadows and Mount Amery.*

The heavy rain that fell all night continued into the morning and rendered the trail, popular with horse parties, a slippery, muddy swathe down which I squelched and slithered past noisy waterfalls, and at one point a busy trail crew trying to improve the tread, for the 9½ miles (15.2km) in pine and spruce forest to bridged Poligne Creek and a junction with the Maligne Pass Trail. This trail crosses Poligne Creek many times, but on my walk all of these thankfully were bridged. After 5½ more miles (8.8km) of muddy path, the beautiful flower meadows of Maligne Pass (7,350ft/2,205m) are reached, although the vista is somewhat spoilt by the signs of heavy horse usage. Heavy clouds blocked out the views of the surrounding mountains for me and a thin covering of snow lay on the ground. The date was 1 August.

The first white explorers of the pass and the Maligne Creek Valley, into which the route now descends, were Mary Schaffer and Mollie Adams who came this way with guides and horses in 1908. Mary Schaffer and her friend Mary Vaux, who came on later trips to the region, are commemorated in the names of campgrounds along the Maligne Pass trail. Mary Schaffer's illustrated *Old Indian Trails of the Canadian Rockies*, written in 1911, has been republished under the title *A Hunter of Peace* (The Whyte Foundation) and is an interesting account of her explorations.

The long descent down the Maligne Creek valley starts gradually as the trail winds through a series of scenic meadows, before entering the trees and passing a series of campgrounds, at the first of which, the Mary Vaux Campground, I stayed the night. The rain stayed too, finally petering out at dawn. The trail runs through willow flats, meadows and forest as it continues down the valley to cross the Maligne River on a bridge 14 miles (22.4km) below Maligne Pass. Another 6 miles (9.6km) of walking leads to the roadhead by Maligne Lake.

With a length of 14 miles (22.4km) Maligne Lake is the longest natural lake in the Canadian Rockies and there is a superb view along it to the glacier-draped peaks at its head from the shore near the day lodge (where there is a café and gift shop), which is worth the minor detour needed from the few hundred yard parking lot crossing that connects the Glacier and Skyline Trails. The ease of access has made this one of the most famous beauty spots in the Canadian Rockies.

An easy ascent leads to a crossing of Evelyn Creek and the small Old Horse Campground, just 3 miles (4.8km) from the Skyline Trail trailhead where I set up camp. There is no bear pole at this site which does not mean, as some Dutch back-packers I met here presumed, that there are no bears! They didn't hang their food, although I did and I'd recommend others to do the same. Rain at dawn here was particularly disappointing, as I was particularly hoping for good weather for my walk along the highest trail in Jasper National Park. However, after a prolonged breakfast (always a good tactic when the early morning weather isn't promising!) consumed under the shelter of a large tree, I set

off anyway just as some blue patches appeared in the sky.

As I followed the switchbacks up to open country and Little Shovel Pass (7,350ft/ 2,205m), the clouds lifted. Just before the pass, a couple from Ontario were packing up at the Little Shovel Campground. They caught me up a short while later as I sat on the edge of the vast and beautiful subalpine meadows known as the Snowbowl. After crossing the rich pastures and sparkling streams of this bowl, reputedly a superb ski touring area in winter, the trail climbs up to Big Shovel Pass, at 7,610ft (2,283m). The name comes from an unusual crossing of the pass in 1911 when Jasper outfitters, the Otto brothers built the first trail over the Maligne range and attempted to take a boat over the pass. The snow was too deep for their horses so they dug out a trail with crude shovels made from the nearest trees, hence Shovel Pass. As I neared the pass, I saw a herd of animals crossing a distant slope. Perusing them through the binoculars I could see that they were caribou, an exciting sight as few of these creatures of the arctic tundra, the North American reindeer, are found this far south.

From the pass, the trail contours round open scree-covered slopes to the mountain tarn of Curator Lake, passing *en route* junctions with the Watchtower Basin and Wabasso Lake trails which could be used as escape routes in bad weather (the highest most exposed section of the Skyline still lies ahead) to, respectively, the Maligne Lake Road (8 miles (12.8km)) and the Icefields Parkway (9 miles (14.4)). As I reached the arid shores of Curator Lake, I could see two tiny dots on the horizon that signified hikers at the top of the short but steep ascent to The Notch, a narrow 8,230ft (2,469m) doorway to the summit ridge of Amber Mountain. At The Notch, a superb vista opens up as a huge spread of mountains comes into view to the north, west and south. Prominent in the scene is the white, glacier-clad Mount Edith Cavell,

*Maligne Lake.*

backed by the snowfields and peaks of the Main Ranges and far below the snaking silver thread of the Athabasca River in its dark, forested valley. A great, high level walk follows for the next 3 miles (4.8km), as the trail winds along the ridge with more and more mountains appearing all around.

As the towering ramparts of Mount Tekarra start to loom closer, the trail starts to descend into the bowl east of this peak, switchbacking down to Centre Lakes and reaching timberline just before Tekarra Lake. Less than ½ mile (0.8km) after the lake, the scenic, if somewhat exposed (I say this because a storm during the night woke me a few times here as a gusty wind shook the tent), Tekarra Campground is reached. Unfortunately, the wind did not keep the mosquitoes away.

From the campground it's 8½ miles (13.6km) of descent to the trailhead on the Maligne Lake Road. There are views to the peaks around Jasper townsite, as the trail leads to the Signal Mountain Fire Road, which is followed for the last 5 miles (8km). The trailhead is about 5 miles (8km) from Jasper townsite.

*Mount Tekarra and Skyline Trail scenery.*

## THE ROUTE

| MILEAGE/(KM) | | PLACE | ELEVATION ft | m |
|---|---|---|---|---|
| 0.0 | 0.0 | Norman Creek bridge/Icefields Parkway | 4,725 | 1,417.5 |
| 2.6 | 4.1 | Norman Creek Campground | 7,000 | 2,100 |
| 5.1 | 8.1 | Sunset Pass | 7,100 | 2,130 |
| 8.5 | 13.6 | Pinto Lake | 5,740 | 1,722 |
| 21.3 | 34.0 | Cataract Pass | 8,250 | 2,475 |
| 25.0 | 40.0 | Nigel Pass Trail Junction | 7,000 | 2,100 |
| 26.8 | 42.8 | Boulder Creek Campground | 6,500 | 1,950 |
| 28.8 | 46.0 | Jonas Pass Trail Junction | 6,275 | 1,882.5 |
| 34.9 | 55.8 | Jonas Pass Summit | 7,610 | 2,283 |
| 38.5 | 61.6 | Jonas Shoulder Summit | 8,100 | 2,430 |
| 40.5 | 64.8 | Jonas Cutoff Campground | 6,955 | 2,086.5 |
| 49.9 | 79.8 | Maligne Pass trail junction | 5,770 | 1,731 |
| 55.5 | 88.8 | Maligne Pass | 7,350 | 2,205 |
| 75.9 | 121.4 | Maligne Lake | 5,545 | 1,663.5 |
| 82.5 | 132 | Little Shovel Pass | 7,350 | 2,205 |
| 87.0 | 139.2 | Big Shovel Pass | 7,610 | 2,283 |
| 89.8 | 143.6 | The Notch | 8,230 | 2,469 |
| 94.9 | 151.8 | Tekarra Lake | 6,755 | 2,026.5 |
| 103.5 | 165.6 | Maligne Lake Road | 3,800 | 1,140 |

The trailhead on the Icefields Parkway is by the **Norman Creek bridge** (4,725ft, Mile 0), from where a steep switchbacking trail climbs for 2½ miles and 2,300ft to the extensive meadows that stretch to **Sunset Pass** (7,100ft, Mile 5.1). A long descent follows down to **Pinto Lake** (5,740ft, Mile 8.5). Beyond the lake, the route turns north up a rough trail beside Cataract Creek that leads to a cross-country above-timberline climb to **Cataract Pass** (8,250ft, Mile 21.3) and a steep descent on loose scree to the headwaters of the south fork of the Brazeau River, which is followed still cross-country to a **junction** with the **Nigel Pass Trail** (7,000ft, Mile 25). This trail is taken past the **Boulder Creek** and **Four Point Campgrounds** to a junction with the **Jonas Pass Trail** (6,275ft, Mile 28.8). This trail is followed up to **Jonas Pass** (7,610ft, Mile 34.9) and then more steeply up the ridge to the north to **Jonas Shoulder Summit** (8,100ft, Mile 38.5). Descend from the ridge into the Poboktan Creek valley, which is followed past **Jonas Cutoff Campground** to bridged Poligne Creek and a junction with the **Maligne Pass Trail** (5,770ft, Mile 49.9). This leads back up to **Maligne Pass** (7,350ft, Mile 55.5), from where a long gradual descent leads down the Maligne River valley, past the Mary Vaux and Mary Schaffer Campgrounds to the roadhead at **Maligne Lake**

(5,545ft Mile 75.9). Here, the signed Skyline Trail starts and immediately climbs to bridged Evelyn Creek and the Old Horse Campground and then on past Little Shovel Campground to **Little Shovel Pass** (7,350ft Mile 82.5). After a dip into the flower meadows of the Snowbowl, the trail climbs again to **Big Shovel Pass** (7,610ft Mile 87) and then traverses open slopes to Curator Lake and a steep ascent to the narrow gap of **The Notch** (8,230ft, Mile 89.8) and the summit ridge of Amber Mountain, which is followed for 3 miles, before the trail descends to **Tekarra Lake** (6,755ft Mile 94.9). The descent continues to the Signal Mountain Fire Road and a final 5 miles of dirt road walking to **Maligne Lake Road** (3,800ft Mile 103.5).

## MAPS

1:50,000 topographic maps: Cline River; Columbia Icefield; Sunwapta Peak; Southesk Lake; Athabasca Falls; Medicine Lake. National Park 1:200,000: Jasper map.

## RECOMMENDED GUIDEBOOK

*The Canadian Rockies Trail Guide* by Brian Patton and Bart Robinson (Summerthought).

# Mount Robson and the Willmore Wilderness:
## Yellowhead Highway to Grande Cache    166 miles (266km)

*Some element of fear probably lies at the root of every substantial challenge.*

Colin Fletcher    *The Man Who Walked Through Time*

Two remote, little-visited wild river valleys, high passes in both the Front and Main Ranges, the busiest place, the highest mountain and the longest trail in the Canadian Rockies make this superlative route one of contrasts, perhaps the most varied in the book. Weaving a tortuous way northwards, it starts along the rarely-walked Moose River Trail in Mount Robson Provincial Park, then takes a brief diversion to the most popular backcountry destination in the Canadian Rockies, Berg Lake, and the foot of Mount Robson itself, the highest peak in the Canadian Rockies. Much of the popular North Boundary Trail is then traversed through Jasper National Park to another abrupt change, as the route enters the Front Ranges via Blue Creek and then the remote and little-visited Willmore Wilderness Park.

This is a route for the experienced and self-sufficient wilderness backpacker who can carry a heavy pack and who is confident at route-finding and river fords. There are no supply points on or near the route, so all food has to be carried for a walk that will take most people ten to twelve days and that means a heavy pack at the start. However, this is not a high mountain trek. Most of the walking is on flattish trails in river valleys. Although the trail is easy to follow most of the time, there are many unbridged creek crossings on the Moose River Trail and no trail signs or backcountry campgrounds, except for those created by horse parties. The same applies to the last 40 or so miles (64km) in the Willmore Wilderness Park, although here the creek crossings are not so deep or difficult as those along the Moose River Trail. The trails however, mostly made by packhorses, are not as distinct. Permits are only required for the section in Jasper National Park, also the only section where backcountry campgrounds are provided and **must** be used.

The rewards of the trip are a real feeling of remote wilderness combined with a wide variety of animal and plant life, as well as scenery. Only at Berg Lake and perhaps along the North Boundary Trail (NBT) will many people be encountered and the chances are that you won't meet anyone along the Moose River or in the Willmore Wilderness. I didn't, even though I walked the route in August, at the height of the backpacking season.

At the start of the route, between the busy trans-Rockies Yellowhead Highway and the tracks of the CNR railway, a map in a glass-fronted case shows the route of the Moose River Trail and marks 'hiker/horse' camps at various intervals. The presence of this map is a

*(Overleaf) The Moose River.*

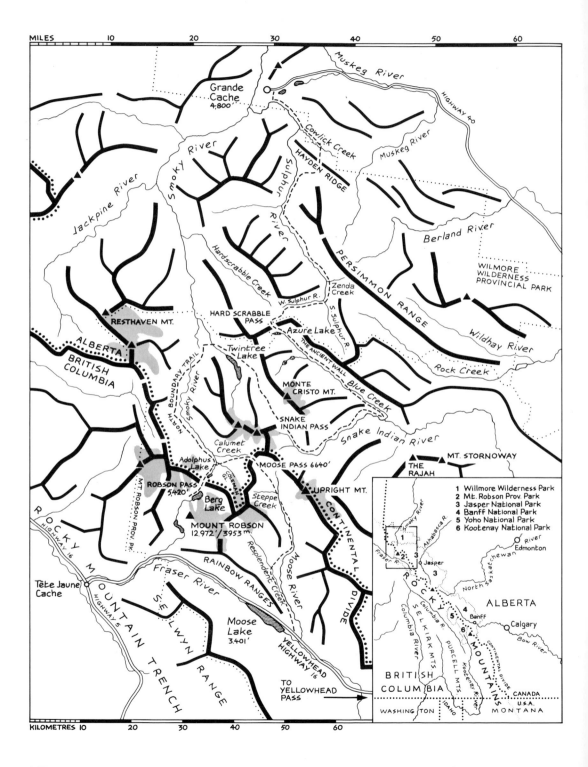

sign that work has been done on the trail with some sections recut, so that it is in far better condition and far easier to follow than as described in the 1986 edition of Patton and Robinson's *Trail Guide* (the work was done in 1988). From the trailhead, a stiff climb leads over the forested but prettily-named Rainbow Ridge and down to the wide, deep, bright blue and slowly flowing Moose River. This pleasant river is followed to Resplendent Creek, a wide, multi-channelled silty stream fed by glaciers that can be seen high up and far away beyond the head of the valley. Nearly 4 miles (6.4km) upstream from its confluence with the Moose River, Resplendent Creek has to be forded. There is a good campsite with a fire-pit on the bank before the crossing, where I stayed and which I would recommend anyone else to stay at if the creek looks at all deep or fast, as glacier-fed creeks are at their lowest early in the morning during the summer, after the glaciers have frozen overnight.

At dawn, Resplendent Creek was no more than ankle-deep. My problem was in finding the spot where the trail resumes on the far bank. It's nearly a mile upstream, so cross at an acute angle (the shingle banks of the river are far easier to walk on than the forested bank) and watch out for a white metal triangle nailed to a tree that marks the start of the trail. Don't do as I did and leave the open flats of the creek until you find the trail. The bank is a dense mat of vegetation and fallen trees and it took me two hours of arduous and frustrating bush-whacking through this jungle before I found the trail, not to be recommended. Once back on the trail another forested ridge has to be crossed before the walk again arrives on the banks of the Moose River. Next, a newly-cut section of trail runs up the valley in and out of the trees, with many good views of the rugged Mount Mackray group. This part of the trail is further away from the river, which is rarely seen, than the old one as described in the *Trail Guide*.

*Mount Robson Provincial Park boundary sign at Robson Pass, with cloud-shrouded Mount Robson behind.*

After around 4 miles (6.4km) the trail does stick closely to the river with four fords in the next 5 miles (8km). Although easy, with a slow-running river, the fords are knee-deep so you might be tempted, as I was, to bushwhack up the bank rather than get your feet wet. Don't succumb! There are good reasons for the fords, in the case of the first, an evil-smelling swamp in which I got my feet wet and my boots muddy. At least the river is clean!

After the fords, Steppe Creek is reached as the valley narrows and the trail is over-shadowed by the peaks to the west, behind which the sun disappears early and with it the heat of the day, as I found when I pounded up the trail in the chill shade of the late afternoon. Two more fords of rather faster and more bouldery Steppe Creek didn't help me to feel warm. Before a third crossing of the creek, lies a rarely-used looking, but pleasant campsite on

a spit of land between the creek and the river where I stopped. I was feeling so cold that I lit a fire for warmth, even though it was mid-August. Dawn brought a clear sky, with many mosquitos and two white-tailed deer that stood and stared at me from a meadow's edge.

A number of trails lead away from the camp-site back to the creek. The crossing is down-stream, *not* upstream where I was inadvertently led by a good track, a diversion that cost me an hour and a half. From the ford, there is a steep climb which levels out as the trees are left behind (there is a nice-looking campsite near timberline) and a long traverse through exten-sive meadows into Moose Pass (6,640ft/ 1,992m), where Jasper National Park begins. The wide pass is surrounded by meadows of purple lupins and other wild flowers, but my enjoyment of these was curtailed somewhat by a cold wind and spots of rain. Away to the

*Mount Robson and the Berg Glacier.*

*The Smoky River.*

*Snake Indian Pass.*

west, heavier clouds were gathering. The trail leads down the Calumet Creek valley and then around the base of a forested spur to a wide, deep and powerful, unnamed creek that is fed by the Coleman Glacier. The crossing of this is by far the most difficult ford of the walk. Downstream of the trail crossing, designed, I imagine, for horses not hikers, the stream spreads out into a·number of channels and it was here I crossed, roaming up and down the shingle banks between each strand of rushing white water looking for the safest way over. Even here the water was thigh-deep, strong and cold. Higher up it was probably impassable. When you have just one channel left, head back upstream to where there is a log bridge, for this last stream is in fact the Smoky River and not the outflow creek. I didn't realize this and spent much futile time searching for a river I'd already forded! A short pull up the bank leads to a junction with the North Boundary Trail. Here, a route decision has to be made.

The through part of the route heads north along the North Boundary Trail. However, just 5 miles (8km) to the south lies Berg Lake and Mount Robson (12,969ft/3,890.7m). It would be a pity to miss seeing the highest peak in the Canadian Rockies when you are so close, so I recommend a diversion to Berg Lake. Less than 2 miles (3.2km) from joining the North Boundary Trail in the direction of Berg Lake is the Adolphus Campground, where I would suggest camping as it is quiet and sheltered and a good base from which to visit the crowded backcountry around Berg Lake. Staying at Adolphus means you can avoid the masses and save having to carry your full pack further than you have to. Also it's free, unlike the three campgrounds that lie over Robson Pass in Mount Robson Provincial Park.

Mount Robson itself first comes into view from the meadows before Adolphus Campground and it was from here that I had my best view of the peak, with just a swathe of clouds, pink-tinged by the setting sun, round its summit. The next day rain fell and grey clouds swirled round the peak. Even in bad weather, the mountain scenery round Berg Lake is worth a visit, if only to see the huge Mist and Berg Glaciers tumbling down from the hidden heights. The popularity of the region means that campfires are forbidden, but there is a day lodge, where hikers can cook and keep warm round the wood stove and store their food, in which I spent a rainy day hoping in vain that the clouds would lift and permit me a longer, closer view of Mount Robson. From the lake, the Berg Lake Trail runs down for ten miles (16km) to the Yellowhead Highway, the shortest escape route from our walk and a fine hike in its own right. This is how most people reach Berg Lake, although for some even this is too far, as I discovered when a helicopter suddenly arrived noisily in the rain to disgorge a party of campers!

The area is dominated by the massive walls of Mount Robson, an awe-inspiring mountain. As befits the highest peak in the range, it is not easy to climb, the most popular route being a four-day mountaineering one involving both ice and rock climbing skills. The mountain was not climbed until 1913, when an Alpine Club of Canada party led by Austrian guide Conrad Kain succeeded after several earlier attempts. The most famous of these was by the Reverend Kinney in 1909 with the assistance of would-be outfitter Curly Phillips, who'd only just arrived from Ontario and had never climbed a mountain before. Despite this, they nearly reached the summit, indeed Kinney claimed they did reach it, but was unable to verify his story. Phillips went on to build the Berg Lake Trail and the boathouse on Maligne Lake (*see* Chapter 9) during his career as a successful outfitter and backcountry guide that ended when he was killed in an avalanche in 1938. *Tracks Across My Trail* by William Taylor (Jasper-Yellowhead Historical Society) tells his

*The shelter at the Berg Lake campsites.*

story and gives the reader an insight into backcountry travel in the early part of the twentieth century.

After my day off at Berg Lake, I headed back across Robson Pass and down the North Boundary Trail. This is the longest single trail in the Canadian Rockies (although it's easy to make longer routes by linking a series of trails), a total of 107 miles (171.2km) from Celestine Lake to the Yellowhead Highway. Due to its length and also the fact that it leads to Mount Robson, it's a fairly popular trail and you can expect to meet a few people every day, especially as the route described here follows the trail away from Mount Robson while people walking the whole of the trail usually head for the peak. While it has impressive sections, I don't think overall that the NBT is by any means one of the better trails in the Rockies, which is why it doesn't have a chapter to itself. However, the 60 miles (96km) of it that we do follow take in all its highlights and provide a convenient, pleasant and relatively easy middle section for

our route, linking the wilder, remoter Moose River valley and Willmore Wilderness areas.

From Adolphus Campground the NBT is followed, mostly in forest, past several campgrounds to a bridged crossing of the Smoky River and then Twintree Lake, where I was treated to a split in the clouds and shafts of sunlight bringing to cold, silver life the dull waters of the lake. The forest that lines most of the NBT is left behind for the highest section of the trail, 6,625ft (1,987.5) Snake Indian Pass, where on my walk I also briefly escaped the dull, rainy weather that accompanied me along most of this trail and which, perhaps, affected my view of it. The pass provides good views of the heavily stratified peaks of the area and lies in alpine meadows, although the best of the flowers had long gone by 18 August. The country remains partly open and quite scenic beyond the pass, as the trail traverses the wide, marshy valley of the Snake Indian River, first in a south-east and then in a north-east direction to a junction with the Blue

*Willow flats and stratified peaks in the Sulphur River valley.*

Creek Trail. There are several good camp-grounds in this section, and from Three Slides, a good view to the south of the distant glacier-clad Upright Mountain which borders the Moose River valley and is often incorrectly identified as Mount Robson.

At Blue Creek, after 60 miles (96km), and, for me, four days of walking from Berg Lake, the North Boundary Trail is left and we turn up beside Blue Creek. For those who wish to complete the NBT, it's 36 miles (57.6km) more in the forest to the trailhead. I spent my last night on the trail at Blue Creek Camp-ground, where a beautiful rainbow welcomed me. Dawn brought a quick exit when I was startled during breakfast, sitting under a tree in the rain, by a noise in the nearby bushes. I looked up. Twenty feet (6m) away a black bear peered back. I yelled, blew a whistle and hurled a couple of rocks. The bear backed off into the bushes but somehow I sensed it was still there so I did the only thing possible and left at once.

The walk now traverses the whole 21 miles (33.6km) of the Blue Creek valley to Azure Lake at its head, a marvellous walk, mostly in open meadows and willow-thicketed stony flats and under the long, limestone cliffs and serrated crest of The Ancient Wall, a typical Front Range mountain ridge. As I progressed up the valley, the clouds slowly dispersed and the rain dwindled to drizzle and then ceased. A cool wind blew down the valley from the north, as bursts of sunlight lit up the meadows. Six-teen miles (25.6km) up the valley, I camped at the Caribou Inn Campground, the last 'official' backcountry site on the route. Just before the site is reached, to the east can be seen the Natural Arch, a curved hole in the folds of Mount Perce, where a huge section of folded strata has eroded away.

Nine miles (14.4km) beyond Caribou Inn, Azure Lake is reached and the trail starts to peter out. However, the line of ascent through a belt of trees and over rocky terraces to the desolate, boulder-strewn broad gap of Hard-scrabble Pass is obvious. Here, spread out before you, are the northern reaches of Jasper National Park and the convoluted strata of the hills of the Willmore Wilderness Park. From the pass, descend eastwards over big slabs of rock with not a tree in sight, soon picking up a pack trail that continues down into the valley of the West Sulphur River. In sunshine, this is a glorious valley, the light-coloured rock walls of the surrounding ridges giving an air of lightness and freedom to the atmosphere, in stark contrast to the gloom of the confining forests of the North Boundary Trail.

The actual routes of the trails in the Will-more Wilderness do not correspond too closely with those marked on the maps and there are far more trails than the map shows, but this hardly matters for our route as long as you stay in the Sulphur River valley. The trail wanders

downstream through dense, low willow thickets under the curving cliffs of the Front Ranges. After the confluence of the West Sulphur with the South Sulphur River, there are several knee-deep fords, but none difficult. Just after crossing Zenda Creek, there is a large horse packer's camp beside the trail where I camped. (The campsites marked on the map do not appear to all be present on the ground, but again this doesn't matter as there are plenty of others and anyway you can camp where you like in the Willmore Wilderness.) There are occasional trail signs in the area, carved on moose antlers nailed to trees, and one large party had left details of their visit on another antler in the campsite. A cold night, plenty of wood and a well-used fire ring saw me sitting round a blazing fire as the stars came out in a black sky, happy to be alone in the wilderness.

From Zenda Creek, the route continues

*Pack trail, willows and Front Range scenery along the Sulphur River.*

along the Sulphur River valley on a good pack trail to an area of vast meadows around the Sulphur River Cabin, a Forest Service hut used by outfitters, which would make a good emergency shelter in bad weather. Otherwise, there is a nice flat campsite in the woods nearby. Five miles (8km) beyond the cabin and meadows the Sulphur River is left behind for a very steep climb on a good, wide trail, the remains of an old fire road, up Hayden Ridge, a climb that seems interminable, when it comes, as it did for me, at the end of a long day. There is a small camping spot just before the climb starts, which I'd suggest using, leaving the climb for the next morning. Eventually, the twisting route does reach the crest of the ridge to then drop down steeply all the way to a ford of Cowlick Creek, beyond which is a good if well-used campsite in a large aspen grove where I stopped with relief just as darkness fell. It's now just an easy, flat 10-mile (16km) walk on trail and dirt road to the small, modern mining community of Grande Cache, where there are all facilities including buses out of the mountains that connect with services to Jasper and beyond.

## THE ROUTE

| MILEAGE/(KM) | | PLACE | ELEVATION | |
|---|---|---|---|---|
| | | | ft | m |
| 0.0 | 0.0 | Yellowhead Highway | 3,540 | 1,062 |
| 28.7 | 45.9 | Moose Pass | 6,640 | 1,992 |
| 35.0 | 56.0 | Smoky River bridge | 5,300 | 1,590 |
| 40.0 | 64.0 | Robson Pass | 5,420 | 1,626 |
| 41.5 | 66.4 | Berg Lake Campground | 5,400 | 1,620 |
| 43.0 | 66.8 | Robson Pass | 5,420 | 1,626 |
| 62.0 | 99.2 | Junction with Lower Smoky River trail | 4,540 | 1,362 |
| 71.5 | 114.4 | Twintree Lake | 5,110 | 1,533 |
| 80.3 | 128.4 | Snake Indian Pass | 6,625 | 1,987.5 |
| 101.0 | 161.6 | Blue Creek Trail junction | 4,900 | 1,470 |
| 112.9 | 180.6 | Caribou Inn Campground | 5,800 | 1,740 |
| 123.3 | 197.2 | Hardscrabble Pass | 6,800 | 2,040 |
| 131.6 | 210.5 | Zenda Creek/Sulphur River | 5,300 | 1,590 |
| 156.6 | 250.5 | Cowlick Creek | 4,900 | 1,470 |
| 166.0 | 265.6 | Grande Cache | 4,800 | 1,440 |

The roadhead is 300yds down a gravel railway access road that leaves the **Yellowhead Highway** 18 miles west of Yellowhead Pass, near the Moose River bridge (3,540ft, Mile 0). Walk across the railway lines to the signpost marking the start of the Moose River Trail. Follow the trail over Rainbow Ridge and down to the Moose River, then along the riverbank to the ford of Resplendent Creek. From the ford, which exits from the creek well upstream from where it enters, cross another forested ridge and descend again to the Moose River, which is forded four times before Steppe Creek is reached. Ford that creek three times before climbing up to **Moose Pass** (6,640ft, Mile 28.7). Descend alongside Calumet Creek, then take the trail southwards round a ridge to a difficult ford of the Coleman Glacier outflow creek and then a bridged crossing of the **Smoky River** and a junction with the North Boundary Trail. Follow this trail south to **Robson Pass** (5,420ft, Mile 43) and then **Berg Lake** (5,400ft, Mile 41.5). Reverse the route to **Robson Pass**, continuing along the North Boundary Trail to **Twintree Lake** and **Snake Indian Pass**, (6,625ft, Mile 80.3) and then a **junction** with the **Blue Creek Trail** (4,900ft, Mile 101) Take the latter trail up past the **Caribou Inn Campground** to Azure Lake and a cross-country route to **Hardscrabble Pass** (6,800ft). Descend into the West Sulphur River valley, soon picking up a good pack trail. Continue through the willows by the river, to a junction with the South Sulphur River and then **Zenda Creek** (5,300ft, Mile 131.6), where there is a good outfitters' campsite. Stay in the Sulphur River valley on pack trails all the way to Hayden Ridge which is crossed on a steep, winding but wide and clear trail which then drops down to a ford of **Cowlick Creek** (4,900ft, Mile 156.6) and another good outfitters' site. A final 10 miles on level trail leads to the town of **Grande Cache** (4,800ft, Mile 166).

## MAPS

1:50,000 topographic maps: Rainbow; Resplendent Creek; Mount Robson; Twintree Lake; Blue Creek. 1:126,720 topographic map: Willmore Wilderness Park. National Park 1:200,000 topographic map: Jasper.

## RECOMMENDED GUIDEBOOK

*The Canadian Rockies Trail Guide* by Brian Patton and Bart Robinson (Summerthought). Note that the section in the Willmore Wilderness Park is not covered by this guidebook.

# Practical Considerations

*Without sufficient planning about terrain, timing, energy consumption, clothing, food and equipment an outdoorsman risks danger for himself and his party.*

Paul Petzoldt  *The New Wilderness Handbook*

## ACCESS/PERMITS

Although there is free access to all the areas that the walks pass through, some of the Wilderness Areas and all the National Parks require permits for overnight stays and it is often necessary to specify which campsites will be used each night. In very popular areas quotas may be in force. Many agencies require you to collect the permit in person, so that up-to-date information regarding trail conditions, campsites and bear warnings can be imparted. The location of ranger stations issuing permits can be obtained from the relevant national park or national forest headquarters.

## GENERAL LOGISTICS

All the walks start and end at places where there is road access. Some can be reached by public transport, but as services and timetables change from year to year it is best to obtain up-to-date local information as close as possible to when the walk is to take place. If no transport is available, hitch-hiking may well be necessary. I have found that lifts are usually reasonably quickly forthcoming even after emerging from a fortnight in the backcountry!

Restocking with food is the other logistical concern. For walks of up to a week long all food can be carried, but for longer treks this makes for a very heavy load. It is better to resupply along the way. Small stores may not carry

suitable lightweight foodstuffs, so it is preferable to pack your own supplies and mail them to yourself care of General Delivery, at the post office address and zip code of a post office *en route*. Parcels should be marked with a 'hold-by' date.

## SEASONS/WEATHER

Throughout the Western Cordillera of North America, the area in which all the walks are to be found, the weather follows a pattern that is surprisingly consistent. Summers are generally hot and dry, although wetter in the North Cascades and Canadian Rockies than in the Colorado Rockies and the Sierra Nevada, and winters cold and snowy. For walkers, the summer season usually starts by late June, depending on when the last snow melts. Most high level trails are open by mid-July although there may be snow patches left that have to be crossed. Many routes may be passable sooner, although climax avalanches and especially unbridged rivers swollen with snowmelt may make travelling them hazardous.

According to the weather statistics. July is the best month for dry, warm weather. August can be cool and damp and, even if it's warm, thunderstorms are likely. September and early October are cooler, with night frosts, but often dry and clear with superb autumn colours. By late October, snow will be piling up in the mountains making many high level trails impassable.

As July, August and early September are the

*Dawn over Floe Lake, at the start of the Rockwall Trail.*

popular months, by going early or late in the season, the backpacker seeking solitude can avoid the crowds. The John Muir Trail is the most popular trail of those described, yet when I travelled it in late May to mid-June I only encountered four other people. However, the penalty for that solitude was the need to carry and use snowshoes, ice axe and crampons and not to have the security of regular ranger patrols and manned backcountry ranger stations.

# EQUIPMENT

Unlike many mountain regions in Europe, especially the Alps, the North American mountains do not have a hut system. Full backpacking gear is needed for all the walks. It may be possible to manage without a tent in the Sierra Nevada or Colorado Rockies in midsummer, but it is essential in the wetter Cascades or Canadian Rockies and recommended for all regions. A heavy mountain tent capable of withstanding high winds is not necessary, however, as most sites are below timberline and well sheltered. Sleeping bags should be adequate down to −5°C (22°F) lower if for early or late season use, and some form of insulating mat is a necessity. In country where bears may be a problem (*see* page 155 below), such as along the John Muir Trail and in particular in the wetter Canadian Rockies, all cooking and eating must take place well away from the tent, so a sheet of nylon (known as a tarp) can be useful as a cooking shelter when it rains. For the same areas a length of line (60 or 70ft (18 or 21m) is long enough) for hanging up food is required.

Although camp fires are commonly used in many areas (though banned in others), they should be regarded as luxuries due to the amount of damage they cause, both in the scars they leave (an avoidable result, see the book

*Soft Paths* (*see* Further Reading) for details) and the wood consumed. This wood is needed to replenish the soil and as nesting and shelter spots for birds and animals. Prepared fire pits and cut wood are provided in some areas, particularly in the Canadian Rockies, but then, no more fuel than is necessary should be burnt. For cooking, a stove must be carried. The only fuel you can obtain just about anywhere in North America is refined petrol or white gas (often called stove fuel or sold under brand names such as Coleman Fuel), so a stove that will run on this is needed. There are several suitable models available.

Clothing should be adequate for protection against rain, wind and cold although for much of the time shorts and tee-shirt can be worn. The layer system is best, so there is no need for heavy, filled jackets. Fabrics should be lightweight, durable, comfortable, quick drying, warm when wet, easy to wash, 'breathable' and, for outerwear, wind and waterproof. In my opinion, pile and fleece or 'thin' insulating fillings (Isodry, Thinsulate) are best for warmwear; thermal 'wicking' materials such as wool, silk, Dunova, polypropylene, Capilene or similar for underwear, and polycotton for long trousers and windproof jackets. Waterproofs are more comfortable if made from a 'breathable' fabric such as Sympatex or Gore-tex, although the non-breathable ones are just as waterproof and far cheaper. If you want just one jacket to double as wind and waterproof go for a 'breathable' one. Apparently minor items such as hat and gloves can make all the difference between comfort and misery in cold, wet weather and it's worth giving as much attention to your choice of these as you do to your expensive jacket. Socks are particularly important and I like to carry medium weight ones for warm weather, when feet expand, and heavy ones for colder conditions; made from wool in both cases, of course.

I did most of the treks in lightweight footwear (not necessarily boots, I wore running shoes in the Bob Marshall Wilderness and fabric/suede trail shoes in the Cascades) and would recommend this type. Only if much snow is to be expected are heavy mountain boots needed. If they are, then items such as snowshoes or skis, ice axe and crampons will probably be required as well.

Because you will be carrying a heavy load (around 40lbs (18kg)) on any of these treks, your pack will be one of your most important pieces of equipment. From painful experience I can tell you that trying to do a long walk with a badly fitting pack is not to be recommended. These days, so many types of back system exist that it's best to try on several, fully loaded, in a store before you select one. Whether you go for an adjustable or fixed back length, or an internal or external frame, is a personal choice. I've used all of them with success. The important thing is that your pack fits you (like a pair of boots, a pack that is ideal for one person may not be suitable for another so there can be no 'best' model) and that it has a well-padded hipbelt. The packbag should be large so that everything fits easily inside.

No areas require special equipment, though a rope could be needed on early season treks in places where rivers are not bridged and can become dangerous torrents during snowmelt. Such fords are noted in the main text.

# HEALTH/MEDICAL

The big health threat is from the water. Sadly, all water in the areas described, even streams high above timberline, may carry giardia, a parasite which can cause a violent and serious stomach complaint. Boiling water kills giardia (and any other potentially threatening organisms), but is hardly a practical solution. Chemical purification is a more convenient method, although chlorine-based tablets are not adequ-

ate. Iodine tablets such as Potable Aqua do work and are the ones to use. The latest, and perhaps best, method of ensuring drinking water is clean however, is to filter it and there are now a number of lightweight filters available.

To help avoid the spread of giardia and other organisms, great care should be taken with human waste. In particular, if no outhouses are provided toilet sites should be at least 220yds (200m) from any water. Waste should be buried a few inches below the surface, and for digging the necessary 'cathole' I recommend carrying a small plastic trowel (but see the book *Soft Paths* for more details and an argument that in some areas leaving it on the surface is better). Toilet paper should be burned if this can be done safely and the ashes buried. If possible, natural materials (snow is surprisingly efficient and pleasant!) should be used instead. Just beware of poison ivy!

Altitude sickness is possible, especially on the John Muir Trail where the route runs between 10,000 and 14,500ft (3,000 and 4,350m) for much of the way and in the Front Ranges where the route reaches 13,300ft (3,990m). The answer is to acclimatize slowly to higher altitudes.

# BEARS

All the walks take place in country inhabited by black bears. In the Canadian Rockies and, in lesser numbers, the Bob Marshall Wilderness, the larger and more dangerous grizzly bear is also found. Bears are not a problem everywhere, but in grizzly country and where black bears have learnt to raid campsites for food, such as along the John Muir Trail (the route with the worst bear problems), precautions must be taken. Up-to-date information can be obtained from ranger stations and park information offices, and leaflets detailing the

*Camping in the Upper Basin on the Pacific Crest Trail.*

required techniques are often issued with permits. Basically, food must be protected from bears in camp which means hanging it at least 12 feet (3.6m) above the ground and 4 feet (1.2m) below a branch and away from the trunk of the tree. In some backcountry campsites, such as those in the Canadian Rockies national parks and in Tuolumne Meadows on the John Muir Trail, poles or even pulley systems are provided to help with bearbagging food. As it is the smell that attracts bears, it is important to sleep well away from where you cook and eat and where you hang your food and *never* store food in the tent.

On the trail an eye should be kept out for bears and bear sign. If much of the latter is seen (droppings, diggings, scratch marks) and the trail is in thick undergrowth, it may be advisable to make a noise so that you don't come upon a bear suddenly, the most dangerous situation. If you see a bear, stay well away, especially if it is a female grizzly with cubs.

Seventy per cent of known grizzly attacks have been by mothers with young.

While being aware that you are in bear country and taking the necessary precautions, don't let the knowledge that bears are out there ruin your trek. I've walked 7,000 miles (11,200km) in bear country since 1982, 2,000 (3,200km) of them in grizzly country and most of them alone, yet I've only seen one grizzly and ten black bears and have never had any problems.

# HUNTING

Hunting takes place in both the USA and Canada in national forests and wilderness areas, although it's forbidden in national parks. Depending on local game regulations, the season may begin in September or October, although October is usual. If you intend walking in areas used by hunters during the season it would be advisable to wear something bright like an orange hat. People do get shot. During the North Cascades and Front Ranges walks, both of which I did in September, I met many hunters and once had a rifle poked at me through my tent door, although the owner was only asking the way!

## MAPS AND GUIDEBOOKS

I have listed the relevant maps and guidebooks at the end of each chapter. On those walks where I have only listed guidebooks, this is because they contain adequate maps with the trails marked on them. I would recommend carrying guidebooks on the other walks too as the trails are often not marked on the maps.

## A NOTE ON PHOTOGRAPHY

All the walks pass through incredibly beautiful and photogenic scenery and most walkers will carry a camera. While a compact is light and simple to use the possibilities for good photographs are limited. If you want more than snapshots I would recommend carrying an SLR with a couple of lenses. I usually carry two SLR bodies, a 24mm lens and 28–70 and 70–210 zoom lenses plus various filters, the most important of which is a polarizer. These days I carry a lightweight tripod too, although most of the photographs in this book were taken handheld or with an improvised support. I suggest using

*The author on the trail in the Canadian Rockies.*

a slow type of film, and 100 ISO is the fastest I would consider – any faster and grain is noticeable and detail, contrast and colour saturation are lost. The photographs in Chapters 1 to 7 were all taken on Kodachrome 64, those in Chapters 8 to 10 on Fujichrome 50 and 100. Dawn and dusk are the best times for photography and the backpacker is well placed to take advantage of the light then. While on the move it's important to have your camera gear ready to hand, as if it's in your pack you won't take many pictures. I carry mine in padded camera cases, one slung across my body, with the the other fastened on to the pack with smaller items in a bumbag.

# Further Reading

## Literature and Information

Arno, Stephen F. and Hammerly, Ramona P., *Northwest Trees* (The Mountaineers) (Detailed guide to the trees of Northern Oregon and Washington.)

Bradt, Hilary and George, *Backpacking in North America* (Bradt Enterprises) (Good general reference book.)

Cunningham, Bill, *Montana's Continental Divide* (Montana Magazine) (Lavishly illustrated geographical work, with much information on the Bob Marshall and Scapegoat Wildernesses.)

Gadd, Ben, *Handbook of the Canadian Rockies* (Corax) (Definitive, comprehensive and essential.)

Graetz, Rick, *Montana's Bob Marshall Country* (Montana Magazine) (Beautifully illustrated geographical and natural history work.)

Green, David, *A Pacific Crest Odyssey* (Wilderness Press) (Story of a Mexico to Canada walk.)

Hampton, Bruce and Cole, David, *Soft Paths* (National Outdoor Leadership School) (How to enjoy the wilderness without harming it.)

Hargrove, Penny and Liebrenz, Noelle, *Backpacker's Sourcebook* (Wilderness Press) (Book of lists of wildernesses, national parks, guidebooks, etc. Useful for planning.)

Harris, Stephen L, *Fire and Ice: The Cascade Volcanoes* (The Mountaineers/Pacific Search Press) (Detailed descriptions of individual peaks from a geological point of view.)

Herrero, Stephen, *Bear Attacks: Their Causes and Avoidance* (Nick Lyons Books) (Horror stories and practical advice; a good mixture!)

Muir, John, *The Mountains of California* (Doubleday) (The original celebration of the Sierra Nevada.)

Pern, Stephen, *The Great Divide* (Phoenix House) (Story of a Mexico–Canada walk through the Rockies.)

Ross, Cindy, *Journey on the Crest* (The Mountaineers) (Story of a Mexico–Canada walk on the Pacific Crest Trail.)

Schmidt, Jeremy, *Adventuring in the Rockies* (Sierra Club Books) (Good general guide to the Rockies in both the USA and Canada.)

Sutton, Ann and Myron, *The Pacific Crest Trail* (Lippincott) (General description with emphasis on natural history.)

Townsend, Chris, *The Great Backpacking Adventure* (Oxford Illustrated Press) (Contains accounts of Pacific Crest Trail and Continental Divide walks.)

Townsend, Chris, *High Summer* (Oxford Illustrated Press) (Story of the first walk along the whole length of the Canadian Rockies.)

Townsend, Chris, *The Backpackers Handbook* (Oxford Illustrated Press) (Equipment and techniques.)

Watts, Tom, *Pacific Coast Tree Finder* and *Rocky Mountain Tree Finder* (Nature Study Guild) (Useful lightweight guides for the pack.)

Whitney, Stephen, *The Sierra Club's Naturalists' Guide to the Sierra Nevada* (Sierra Club Books) (Natural history guide.)

## Trailguides

Beers, Don, *The Magic of Lake O'Hara* (Rocky Mountain Books)

Darvill, F., *Hiking the North Cascades* (Sierra Club Books)

Dee, Urbick and Spring, Vicky, *94 Hikes in the Northern Canadian Rockies* (The Mountaineers)

George, T., *The Mount Jefferson Wilderness Guidebook* (Solo Press)

Kelsey, Joe, *Climbing and Hiking in the Wind River Mountains* (Sierra Club Books)

Kenofer, L., *Trails of the Front Ranges* (Pruett)

Mitchell, Finis, *Wind River Trails* (Wasatch)

Murray, John *The Indian Peaks Wilderness Area Guide* (Pruett)

Ormes, Robert *Guide to the Colorado Mountains* (Swallow Press)

Patton, Brian and Robinson, Bart, *The Canadian Rockies Trail Guide* (Summerthought)

Rogers, Warren, *Pacific Crest Trail Pocket Guide* (Pacific Crest Club)

Schaffer, Schifrin, Winnett and Jenkins, *The Pacific Crest Trail 1: California* (Wilderness Press)

Schaffer, J. and Selters, A., *The Pacific Crest Trail: Oregon and Washington* (Wilderness Press)

Spring, Ira, *100 Hikes in the Alpine Lakes* (The Mountaineers)

Spring, Ira, *100 Hikes in the North Cascades* (The Mountaineers)

Spring, Ira, *100 Hikes in the South Cascades and Olympics* (The Mountaineers)

Spring, Ira and Manning, Harvey, *Northwest Trails* (The Mountaineers)

Spring, Vicky and King, Gordon, *95 Hikes in the Canadian Rockies* (The Mountaineers)

Starr, Walter, *Starr's Guide to the John Muir Trail and the High Sierra Region* (Sierra Club Books)

Strickland R., *Pacific Northwest Trail Guide* (Wilderness Press)

Winnett, Thomas, *Guide to the John Muir Trail* (Wilderness Press)

Wolf, Jim, *Guide to the Continental Divide Trail: Northern Colorado* (Continental Divide Trail Society)

Wolf, Jim, *Guide to the Continental Divide Trail: Northern Montana* (Continental Divide Trail Society)

Wolf, Jim, *Guide to the Continental Divide Trail: Wyoming* (Continental Divide Trail Society)

# Index